Return from Nowhere

Return from Nowhere

A mother's struggle against the system

Claire Byrne

Fern House

First published in 2012 by
Fern House, Haddenham, Cambridgeshire CB6 3XA
www.fernhouse.com

© Copyright Claire Byrne 2012
All rights reserved

The right of Claire Byrne to be identified as the author
of this work has been asserted by her in accordance with
the Copyright, Designs and Patents Act 1988

ISBN-13 978-1-902702-30-8

Design: istudio21, Cambridge
Printing: QNS, Newcastle upon Tyne

Contents

	Preface	1
1	1990 – A World Cup nightmare	5
2	Bureaucracy and wasted days	11
3	Blind alleys	21
4	Struggle, hardship and a new hope	35
5	Concrete hopes	52
6	Rehabilitation?	63
7	Out of the quicksand?	98
8	Progress despite frustrations	118
9	The carer's tale	132
10	Operation NHS	149
11	Against my better judgement	170
12	Shifting sands	191

Preface

It might give us comfort to believe that health professionals have our best interests at heart, and that the healthcare and general care systems are designed to maximise the chances of favourable outcomes when we need them the most. But unfortunately it is precisely when we do need them the most that we are at our lowest points, and this gives the incompetent the opportunity to benefit financially and in reputation. They can write off 'hopeless cases' and take no blame for their failure while reaping the rewards of successes that have taken place – sometimes incidentally or despite their opposition – under their management.

Claire's story is just one example of how things can go wrong. It all started when her son David suffered a brain haemorrhage while on holiday abroad in 1990. The local healthcare providers' failure to take the situation seriously turned out to be a depressing taste of things to come, as his first contact with an NHS specialist was to prove. By the time the seriousness of the damage was recognised, it was too late, and David was on the path to needing life-long care. Early intervention in the UK, even given the time that had elapsed between the incident and his arrival, could have removed the threat of permanent damage and put David on the road to recovery and a return to a full and productive life, although the recovery would have been at a snail's pace, even with the full support required.

It became clear that David was now completely reliant on Claire. As she tried to overcome the many obstacles placed in her path by the healthcare provision and benefits agencies, just to pursue a medical negligence case, she was forced to confront abuse and murder in care establishments and pomposity and personal insults from the upper echelons of the professions. Through the worst years, David needed

24-hour care and would act unpredictably, flitting between threats of violence, bouts of forgetfulness and a tendency to be inappropriately affable with strangers. Claire's own life inevitably became a mere backdrop, with her health suffering as sleep, food and work were sacrificed.

But perseverance, determination and the development of a healthy disrespect for authority would eventually force Claire through the headwind that would have swept less dogged mothers away. She took on the powers-that-be – and won – forcing the medics, administrators and lawyers to back down from their attempts to control someone they variously judged to be a pushover and a golden goose. The story illustrates the lengths to which people will go to boost their own esteem and line their pockets, but it also shows how preying on the vulnerable could be potentially profitable for any group that can close ranks and play the system.

The story is as inspirational as it is heartbreaking, and as we follow Claire through the highs and lows of her lost decade we cannot help but feel a respect for, and empathy with, her. Perhaps even her erstwhile adversaries feel the same way now that the dust has settled; perhaps she has made them change the way they treat people in their professional and private lives. Or perhaps not.

It is important to point out that this story is not an attack on the medical profession. As well as being the initiators of many of her woes, it is also the profession that diagnosed David and eventually helped to bring him up to the level he occupies today, with a degree of independence. It is, however, an attack on arrogance, advantage-taking and turning a blind eye to abuses of power, and that goes to the very highest levels of society.

* * *

Claire has spent many years caring for David, and although she is still based with him in his home, she is now firmly in the background, granting him as much freedom and independence as possible. She is now able to disappear every so often to spend time with her partner George at his holiday home, and is looking forward to maybe spending some months each year away, lapping up the sun and enjoying life.

Preface **3**

David will certainly be joining her during some of those trips, as he loves the place nearly as much as they do.

But Claire could not rest until her story had been told. She recognised that David had, despite everything, been lucky that the dice that had been tumbling for ten years settled exactly as they did. This book is dedicated to the memory of the many others who were less fortunate than her son, in the hope that it will be of some benefit to others in the future.

So, at last, Claire's story is told, and she can have peace of mind. Whether or not anything will change, she doesn't know; what she does know is that, until people start giving those who need care the care that they deserve, nothing will change, so if this can save just one person from going through a living hell, her efforts will have been worthwhile.

Perhaps she can now begin to wake up from the nightmare, rub her eyes and look to the future.

Charlie Hankers
May 2012

1

1990 – A World Cup nightmare

As I was saying goodbye to my sons, David and John, I could sense another step in their growth into young men, as though they were stretching out and finding their feet in the world. This was no ordinary goodbye. For John, then eleven years old, it was his first holiday without his mother. His 22-year-old brother was taking him abroad, and the excitement of both was palpable. It was, I suppose, a bittersweet farewell to those memorable family holidays whose images fill photo albums and whose souvenirs sit on shelves and eventually end up at the backs of drawers from where they might, sometime in the future, during a spring clean or while scrabbling around to find a working pen, re-emerge to raise a smile.

Worry was not on my mind; I had, I hoped, brought up two level-headed sons, and I had every faith in David's ability not only to look after John, but also to make sure that the pair of them had the time of their lives.

And what a time it was to go abroad; this was late June 1990, and for anyone remotely interested in football, that means the World Cup in Italy. The heady imagery speaks for itself: Cameroon beating Argentina, David Platt's goal against Belgium, Paul Gascoigne's tears, and the cup finally being held aloft by West Germany, shortly before reunification.

David was, by any measure, a football fanatic. He had loved kicking balls about for longer than he could remember and, although academically he was never brilliant, he had proudly played for schools' teams throughout his education. He was even considered talented enough for a trial for Whitely Athletic though sadly he never joined the squad. But he continued to play Sunday League football and took employment instead with the local council. So holidaying during Italia

6 *Return from Nowhere*

'90 in the sultry climate – a break from the mundanity of work and a chance to watch the epic battles on the pitch – was heaven on earth for him. Only England returning home as world champions could have made it sublime.

However, by the time Chris Waddle was considering where in the Stadio delle Alpi he should place his penalty, David would have more important things on his mind.

* * *

There is plenty to occupy the mind of a 22-year-old beside the pool in a holiday hotspot; indeed, David might even have put Bobby Robson's choice of first eleven momentarily to the back his mind as he relaxed with his brother and soaked up the relentless rays. The jollity of life was buzzing and splashing from every direction, and his tan, that delightful work in progress, was tingling away nicely. His younger brother was enjoying himself in his own way, cooling off in the pool and generally lapping up the freedom and fun of this typical British holiday – no doubt his first of many.

After several hours in the hot sunshine, the Whitely constitution started to reveal itself, and David realised that a short break was in order. He had developed a throbbing headache and had started to feel dehydrated. Knowing that the hotel grounds were secure and that there were plenty of people around, he had no worries about leaving John down by the pool on his own. They arranged to meet up an hour later by the pool, and his little brother trotted back happily to the water.

David let himself into his room and set his shower to a temperature as far away as possible from the furnace he had been lying in. He had associated his headache with the heat, and reasoned that the opposite – a fresh, chilled jet of water – would cure it so that before long he could be back in the sun.

The next moment changed his life.

Whether it was a simple slip on the smooth, wet floor or the shock of the rapid change in temperature is not clear; but a fraction of a second later David was snatching viciously towards the marble slabs that had moments earlier been so pleasurable underfoot. His head cracked against their unyielding surface and in an instant he lost consciousness.

The planned hour passed, and John was sitting around waiting for David to come and meet him. After several glances at the clock he shook his head in despair. "What is he up to now?" he thought, and tutted as petulantly as any pre-teen would at such an inconvenience.

David had by now come round, but far from being cured, the throbbing in his skull had now become an unbearable, agonising pain. Water continued to sprinkle on him from above, but when he instinctively tried to get up and switch it off, he realised that the left side of his body would not respond to the commands his brain was giving it; he was suffering partial paralysis and was wracked with terror. How long would John wait before coming up? Did anyone else know he was here?

Agonisingly, painstakingly, he dragged his limp self towards the bed. This, he was still thinking, was the worst case of sunstroke he had ever had. Every tentative movement of his body made his nervous system scream at him to stop. But he knew that a good lie down would do him the world of good, and he carried on towards the visibly cool bed sheets, trying to work out how he could hoist his body up on to the mattress when only half of it was working.

If you've never had a brain haemorrhage before, how on earth are you supposed to know what it feels like? How can you hope to realise that every second, blood is leaking from its vessels and putting more pressure on your brain, and that every minute you spend without emergency medical assistance shortens your life expectancy, potentially to just a few hours into the future? The answer is – you can't. You do what you've always done when you're not well – you head for bed and wait for everything to sort itself out.

How long should you wait for someone to come? If you wait for five minutes and then leave, they will almost certainly come and miss you. If you wait for fifteen minutes, they could still have been delayed. If you wait for an hour, they may have forgotten, fallen asleep, or ... no, you don't want to think about anything else. With a final, irritated look at the clock – but also a dawning sense of concern for his brother who, being eleven years his senior, had something of an avuncular relationship to him – John did what he saw as the sensible thing and headed back to the hotel room where he knew David was going when they had parted.

On entering the room John saw his brother lying in bed and sighed. But immediately he sensed something was not right. Never had David been so pleased to see him, but when John started asking questions, the answers that came from David's mouth were just confused ramblings. By now, thankfully, the paralysis had receded and he could gingerly move his left arm, but the intense ringing from inside his skull had got no better.

Somehow David managed to let John know he needed medical help, and by a miraculous summoning of strength, the two of them, looking for all the world like a drunk dad and his embarrassed son, made it down to the hotel reception to be greeted with seen-it-all-before smiles from the staff, who advised them to go to the local clinic. A taxi was called.

Their first sight of the clinic hardly filled the brothers with optimism. The unclean and ramshackle building might have been mistaken for a condemned hovel, were it not for the broken red cross swinging above the door. The clinician couldn't understand English too well, but knew straight away what was wrong and delivered his expert diagnosis: sunstroke. Examination was hardly necessary; it was obvious. What else could a British tourist be afflicted with? Frostbite? No, there was no doubt about it. Treatment: pain killers and a good night's sleep. Prognosis: back by the pool tomorrow afternoon. This was not a reasoned examination; it was the voice of experience, otherwise known as arrogance. The doctor jabbed a pain killer into David's arm and sent him on his way, after the financial matters had been dealt with.

Back they taxied to the hotel, every bump of the ill-maintained road network shooting like a bolt into David's brain. The same staff joked with them on arrival, and wished him well after his sleep. Despite the incessant agony that was afflicting David, he still felt like he had to keep up a front and try to appear as normal as possible, to laugh it off, to alleviate the embarrassment of being naïve enough to stay outside in thirty-degree heat when his natural habitat was among fresh Pennine raindrops.

Only John noticed that all was not well, but he had to listen to the advice of adults.

1990 – A World Cup nightmare	**9**

The sleep that the doctor ordered proved desperately impossible, yet was all that David yearned for. Nausea had become ever-present along with the head pains, stomach cramps and weakness that played their roles in making that night a sleepless one. The next day no improvement looked likely, and the brothers decided a doctor needed to be called; another trip to the clinic was as impossible as it was futile.

Eventually a real, proper, fully qualified doctor arrived at the hotel room. Again, no relevant or substantial test was done as the medic had presumably used the same tools of diagnosis as the clinician – age, sex, and race stereotypes. And, indeed, his opinion mirrored that of the clinic: it was sunstroke. Another injection, another recommendation that David rest, another bill to be paid.

Another sleepless night; insomnia was becoming as much a strain on his being as was the pain. Inevitably, blackouts followed.

The third day dawned. A third doctor was sought. A third sunstroke diagnosis was given. This time David refused the ineffectual injection, possibly saving a few pesetas from the bill.

For five days, David simply lay in bed, hoping for an improvement that would prove never to come. Desperation gave way to depression and hopelessness. David could see no future. He doubted if he would ever make it off the island. Was he supposed to get on a plane like this? How would the cabin pressure affect him? Did he have to endure another taxi journey to the airport while every pothole and corner would exacerbate his nausea and pain? For a serene moment he thought none of this would matter. Because he thought he was going to die.

He made it to the end of his holiday in the sun. They had paid for and made use of all the boxes ticked on the travel agent's form. His slot in this particular room in this hotel was over, and by this time tomorrow someone else would be lying in this bed, full of plans for a fortnight of sun, sea and sand. It took hours, but the two of them packed their cases and made it down to the waiting taxi, David once again putting on his normal guy act. But inside he just wished he could project himself several hours into the future and not have to endure the discomfort of air travel that awaited him.

10   *Return from Nowhere*

The beginning of the flight proved much better than either brother had dared to imagine. The optimism of being homeward bound buoyed him and the positive motion of the plane heading north made every mile seem a light year away from hell and a step nearer paradise.

But this was short-lived. Before long his condition deteriorated and he started to suffer spasms. One particularly unfortunate leg twinge sent his food tray flying onto the floor; the passengers stopped what they were doing and stared accusingly at David. No doubt they just saw another Englishman abroad, drunk on Duty Free and prone to violence.

Moments later the stewardess arrived and David and his brother spent the rest of the flight sitting right at the rear of the plane, to prevent distress to other passengers.

The idea that immediate medical help should be sought, or that an ambulance should be waiting on the tarmac, never occurred to anyone.

Meeting the brothers at the airport was me, the mother who had a fortnight ago so cheerfully seen them on their way.

What I saw made me shudder. Coming towards me was a limping, struggling David, emaciated but with a bloated face and swollen head, being propped up by John. John ran towards me and gave me a kiss, saying that David was not well. He made it sound like a stomach bug, and I thought my eyes must have been deceiving me, but as David hobbled ever closer it became clear that something was terrifyingly amiss.

I set off straight to Brookside General Hospital as my sons, mainly John, recounted what had happened.

Perhaps a correct diagnosis awaited David at last.

2

Bureaucracy and wasted days

My initial instincts seemed to have exhibited infinitely more insight than all of the so-called medical experts who had failed David up until this point. It was close to unbelievable that nobody had thought for even a second that his problem might have been more serious than was being suggested. This was not maternal intuition or even familiarity with David's normal behaviour – it was pure common sense.

We arrived at Brookside General Hospital and sat impatiently in the waiting room. David's spasms continued with alarming frequency and intensity, so much so that even other people waiting for treatment watched aghast as this young man's uncontrollable bodily jolts, kicks and contortions became the centre of attention. A wheelchair was produced as if by magic and there was unspoken agreement between the patients and those accompanying them that David's need was more urgent than their own; when someone's name was called, they volunteered that David should precede them. The reaction of these non-medical members of the public is further evidence that the blatancy of David's plight had been ignored or overlooked previously.

The junior doctor immediately knew that the horrific symptoms before him were not caused by sunstroke. For the first time it was suggested that a brain haemorrhage was responsible, but there was a series of tests to undergo before any useful conclusions could be reached. At last, David received his first proper medication, and he was admitted overnight for observation.

I clearly remember asking the doctor if David was going to die. It is the sort of sentence you never imagine yourself uttering in relation to your son. He reassuringly replied in the negative.

The following morning there would be a scan and an appointment with a specialist neurosurgeon, all of which would require a transfer to the much better equipped Victoria General Hospital.

The ambulance journey was a nerve-wracking experience. Who knew what conclusions would be arrived at? But even if the diagnosis was bad, at least a clear picture of the appropriate treatment could be built up. A positive outlook is the only way to get through such traumas; as a family we were, at best, hopeful that the beginning of some effective treatment was approaching.

At the Victoria General Hospital a CT brain scan was performed, and the cause of David's incapacity became much clearer. A haemorrhage was now all but certain to be the root, and further confirmation came in the shape of an alarming bout of weakness, when David could barely muster the strength to move a muscle.

He was transferred to the Acute Head Injury Ward and we were told that a two-week period of observation was required. This sounded like hell to David, who longed to be at home where he would be comfortable and secure; it was beginning to feel like months since he had walked out through the front door to go on his fateful holiday. After a brief moment of consideration, Mr Winner, the Consultant Neurosurgeon, said David could go home, provided that he was given complete rest, was not left alone for a moment and would be brought back for further tests two days later. We agreed in an instant.

Furthermore, no action could be taken until the results of the tests had been returned to Mr Winner – and that meant no operation, no attempt to treat the cause of David's intense pain and involuntary spasms, just some medication to alleviate the agony somewhat.

Back in the safety of the home and with the love of his family, David visibly relaxed, despite the evident distress he was in, the type that could make even observers flinch with shock. But even this was more tolerable than his being cooped up on a ward; at least now he was with people who knew him, whom he trusted.

Three days later, on 17 July, he was taken back to hospital for the further tests, a lumbar puncture and an ECG. This time there was no option to go home, so he stayed on the ward for two more days before he could return to his own bed. This was a grim and shocking place, to say the least. As I walked along the aisle towards David, I passed bed after bed of despair: motionless shells of people with shaven heads; tubes squirting and sucking unidentifiable liquids though orifices and punctures; wires; machines; signs saying 'nil by mouth'; graphs; and echoes. The first time there I did not even make it to David's bed. I turned on my heel as I felt an intense nausea. I remembered seeing a bin in reception and made it just in time to be sick into it. I was embarrassed and felt guilty; a nurse told me that mine was in fact quite a common reaction among first-time visitors.

A week later he was back again, this time for a cerebral angiogram and a stay as an in-patient at the Acute Head Injury Ward.

At last, there was no doubt about David's condition – the fact that he had suffered a brain haemorrhage was now certain. This was a momentous revelation, and you would assume that the journey to recovery had been embarked upon. After all, now there was a concrete diagnosis, treatment would be a matter of routine – wouldn't it?

We were brought down to earth in the efficiently stoical manner practised by all medical practitioners. The news was far from positive. Haemorrhages need to be treated immediately if they are to be effectively stemmed or for their effects to be minimised. The emergency services' maxim that seconds save lives is acutely true in this case; every millilitre of escaping blood takes the victim a tiny bit closer to a tipping point whose moment in time – and whose consequences – are unknowable. By this point, of course, a fortnight had passed.

Although David was undoubtedly lucky to be alive, the passage of time had caused the haemorrhage to seal itself over, which left him in something of a limbo.

Attempting to operate on the wound at this stage could, it was considered, make matters worse, as the exact spot of the wound could not be ascertained. It is always much better to operate on a haemorrhage while it is in its initial phases.

Then the chilling message was delivered – that the chances of a second haemorrhage taking place were 100 per cent.

These two factors, taken together, left medical experts with a clear conclusion: the best time to operate would be when David's brain started bleeding again.

It was a case of enduring a terrifying wait for the inevitable to happen. Even Bond villains have the gallantry to leave a visible countdown clock on their time bombs. David could not even guess at the month during which his own calamity would strike.

So then came the next shock to our family. David was told that he simply had to get on with his life until he was struck again. That meant going back to work, going back to his daily routine and, yes, back to his beloved football team – with the unbelievably reckless proviso that he did not head the ball. Surely if nodding a leather ball of compressed air was more than his fragile head could take, the idea of indulging in any type of contact sport should have been out of the question. It seemed like common sense was not something the overeducated specialist was blessed with.

The waiting stage began. How a person is supposed to even attempt to continue along life's daily trail with such a looming horror is anyone's guess. But David gave it his best shot. There were spells of dizziness, forgetfulness, insomnia, clumsiness, fear and helplessness to contend with, but underpinning it all was a determination to get on with it that was a credit to his fortitude. He was under 24-hour supervision; not a moment could pass when he was not with at least one person who knew of his condition – and knew that if the first signs of the inevitable re-emergence of the haemorrhage surfaced on their watch, they would be in the centre of a life-or-death emergency situation, and that David had to be taken straight to Victoria General Hospital, the closest place available with the required specialist equipment and personnel.

He tried to work, but was not exactly effective in his physically demanding job. He was put on light duties, but even this was hopeless for someone who would regularly suffer severe headaches and fatigue with any physical exertion, and loss of feeling down the left-hand side of his whole body. He was confused and frightened at this time as he did not understand what was happening to him. He was disoriented, always on edge, assuming that every sensation that he felt inside his head was the first heaving rumble of the storm to come. But as these alerts passed and with the knowledge that the second attack was inevitable absorbing every waking moment, merely living was becoming a traumatic and tiring experience. His workmates and superiors simply could not believe that the specialist had considered him fit for work. But who would question such a person? Of course, everyone at work was drilled with the emergency procedure. This thing could come at any moment. When it did, swift action was vital.

On 1 September, his sporting urges got the better of him. For someone who had eaten and slept football since childhood, his involuntary separation from the excitement of the pitch and the camaraderie of the team was proving too much for him to take. He had started to wonder if turning up for a game might actually do him the world of good. Perhaps deep inside, he was inspired by the idea that the activity could have triggered the dreaded – yet perversely longed-for – event. Who knows?

So he made his unsteady way back to the pitch. It was a short comeback. A feeling of illness like nothing he had experienced before gripped him. He stopped dead in his tracks, the noises of the game continuing as though behind a muffling wall. He felt dizzy and was very unsteady on his feet; he was disoriented and needed help to return home. This was it. It had started.

David was taken back to his home, from where I was telephoned by the person who had taken him there, pleading to get him to hospital. I arrived home to see my son collapsed in the doorway, unable to move or speak coherently. He was paralysed from the neck down, and merely swung his head and made unrecognisable, horrific noises. I called an ambulance.

As is the way with emergency calls, the closest Accident and Emergency is prepared to receive the patient. Because of geographical proximity to our home, this was deemed to be the Whitely Hospital. When the ambulance arrived, I gave the paramedics clear instructions that David had to be taken to Victoria General Hospital, where they had the specialist unit and were expecting him at some point. The driver shook his head and uttered some bureaucratic stuff about where he could and could not take patients.

"OK," I insisted, infuriated, "Help me carry my son to the car. I'm taking him to the Victoria General myself."

The paramedics looked at each other for a moment and decided to radio base, then returned with the news that they could take David to where he needed to be. More seconds were being wasted. This was not looking good. Fair enough, one fewer ambulance in Whitely could have proved fatal had other accidents taken place during the detour, but perhaps discretion should have played a more prominent role here. I hoped that this occurrence would result in a meeting, a directive, a recommendation, a clause, a procedural rethink, a policy shift or a note on the agenda of the next advisory body's seminar – but in all likelihood it did not cause so much as a ripple of discontent. It was only now that I realised how much danger the surgeon's instruction had put David in. I am sure that many of those charged with looking after him might not have insisted, in the heat of the moment, on his being taken to Victoria General Hospital rather than the closest Accident and Emergency hospital. I followed the ambulance as best I could in my car. Of course, it was jumping red lights and speeding skilfully along, while I was barely able to see through the tears that were continually welling up in my eyes. The ambulance carrying my son soon left me behind, and somehow I managed to complete the journey without requiring another ambulance to be sent out.

For the moment, the most important thing was getting David to the right place, where life-saving intervention could commence.

At least he was heading in the right direction.

* * *

On arrival at the Victoria General Hospital, David was put in a cubicle and I had to go and sit in a waiting room. In sharp focus among the fuzzy and confusing goings on, I still clearly remember the forlorn sight of a young child rubbing dirt into his face from his filthy hands, his mother, an unkempt and waif-like older female version of him, looking on. The man I assumed to be her husband was pacing back and forth, ignorant of both of them. The child was crying and asking for something to eat. In response the mother was saying, purposely loud, that there was nothing to eat because daddy had lost all the money at the bookies.

The receptionist announced that the police had been called and that they should go home. The mother said she had no home, for the same reason that they had no food. For the first time I saw the father's face; it was emaciated and freshly scarred and his head was shaven. It was a depressing scene, and my bit part in it ended when I was called to the cubicle.

I was told that David was to be placed in the Neurological Ward. I was glad that he had a place to go to, but then shocked to hear that it would specifically be the Acute Head Injury Unit rather than straight into the operating theatre. Mr Winner had said that emergency surgery would be essential on the occasion of the second haemorrhage, so why was this not happening? Not for the first time I put my son's welfare in the hands of a medical professional. I did query Mr Winner, but he practically rolled his eyes at me and made a sarcastic comment about which of us knew best what to do. I apologised, of course. That is what you do.

The 'emergency' surgery – for which all of David's family and acquaintances had been put on red alert and for which an ambulance had been called and diverted – was to take place a whole five days later after the results of further tests. In the interim I became extremely irritated by the seeming lack of action on David's case, and pestered and questioned Mr Winner and his colleagues on every possible occasion. I was continually fobbed off with assurances that he was in the best possible hands, and despite my growing misgivings, I eventually said I would trust in his judgement.

I was not so sure, of course.

Over the following days, the paralysis receded a little, although David was nowhere near being back to his state from a few days earlier, let alone that of before the first haemorrhage.

"Sign this," Mr Winner said abruptly, handing me a consent form to sign. In my emotional state, I could not take in the words of the form, so understanding them was out of the question. I started to panic and asked what would happen if the operation was not performed. "David will die," he replied. "In fact, even with the surgery there is no guarantee of a successful outcome, and by successful I mean that he will survive but will forever need a wheelchair or could have other disabilities."

The fact is that only days earlier, David and I had discussed what I should do if I had to make the decision to let him live or die, if living meant that he would no longer be able to play football and do the things he loved. He had made it known that if the risk was high, I should let him go, and should not carry my decision around with me all my life; in essence, that I should be able to remember him as the athletic and happy young man he had been. He was referring to the people who had so shocked me in the Unit, the staring, motionless ones with wires and tubes sustaining them. I had told him that that would go against everything I believed in, that he must have been meant to survive or he would have been dead already. Surely he had to be given every chance medical science, nature and fortune could offer him? I told him that Mr Winner was the best there was, despite a less than perfect bedside manner. I changed the subject. The next time I had seen my son he had taken a pre-med and was drifting in and out of consciousness, yet forced himself to stay awake long enough to await my arrival, upon which he reiterated his desire to die rather than go on living as what he could only see as being an empty shell.

With all this in my mind, I had to make a decision. The form was being brandished under my nose, and an impatient Mr Winner was holding it. "Okay," I said, and signed it. For some reason I trusted him. Seconds later he was gone. On 6 September, David finally went in for his surgery, a right frontal craniotomy and the clipping of the aneurysm. For the next hours I was in torment, wondering what was going on in theatre.

* * *

The days following the operation were among the worst so far. His recovery was progressing very slowly, and the things I saw on the ward made me doubt he was receiving adequate care. It seemed as if people there were neglected, or at best given the absolute minimum of attention. I was convinced that just before visiting time, when concerned friends and relatives would turn up, was the only time the patients in the ward were seen to. I say this without meaning to criticise the nursing staff, who were all dedicated and caring, but desperately overstretched. I visited every day, even though I was told that this was not necessary.

But this was my son, and I had to make sure that everything was being done for him.

Gradually, his condition improved from the absolute low he had endured after the operation. But these were not comfortable times by any means. He was suffering from excruciating pain in his left calf, and the agony he felt in his chest made every breath torturous. When this latter condition became particularly bad during one of my visits, I alerted the nurses several times because I was convinced that he was suffocating, such were the deathly gasping sounds he was making. I did notice that after my first request the staff became short with me and got annoyed, insisting that the doctor was on his way. It took twenty minutes for him to arrive, and he prescribed some intravenous anticoagulation medication. I would later discover from an expert that the dosage he was given was in fact useless.

During September on one of my visits to the hospital, a case with echoes of David's was creating a highly charged atmosphere in the reception. I had been forced to sit there with the other visitors by a particularly arrogant consultant who insisted that no visitors were allowed to be present during his rounds. On this occasion the victim was a 26-year-old named Paul who had fallen down some stairs after drinking, but who had not received the attention he should have when he complained of a headache. It turned out that he too had suffered a brain haemorrhage, but no doubt the scent of alcohol on his breath had caused those who initially dealt with him to skip the precautionary tests for haemorrhage and diagnose a hangover, recommending paracetamol with disastrous results. On this occasion, it was his parents who were abroad, however, and the waiting room was awash with tears as the friends and family tried desperately to contact them but to no avail. Paul's loved ones had actually been told to go and pay their last respects to him. It suddenly dawned on me that the lack of imagination exhibited by the doctors abroad was not restricted to their part of the world. Based on this admittedly small sample, you could start to wonder if head injuries are ever taken seriously when accompanied by alcohol, the sun or national stereotypes of Britons abroad.

As September wore on, David's condition did start to improve, albeit at an agonising slow pace. At the end of the month he was allowed home for the weekend to see how he coped, and when it was considered safe, he was discharged. It was now early October.

We were all relieved, indeed elated, to have David back home for good, because we were in no doubt that we were at last starting to wake up from the nightmare. We knew that he had had a serious condition and a dangerous operation, and that we would need patience and perseverance, but we prepared ourselves for the coming months with optimism and determination.

Had I known then that recovery would take seventeen years, perhaps I would have been a little more reflective about the situation.

Whenever I am describing David's story to people who are new to it, they are usually disturbed, sympathetic by this point, and if they know David or me personally, they can also be quite emotionally drained and immensely sympathetic; but they are always glad that the story ends happily. That is because in a normal story, the beginning, the middle and the end would by this stage have been covered, the happy conclusion reached.

So when I tell listeners that this is the stage of the story that I usually consider to be the *beginning*, they cannot be blamed for the surprise they always fail to conceal.

3

Blind alleys

I had been told that, with care and attention, David would eventually be able to lead a normal life, and that after a period of rest and recuperation, our initial aim should be to work together to get David back to work as soon as possible. Of course, I had nodded along, making mental notes about what would be the procedure for the following weeks and perhaps months: care, love, attention and occasional professional assistance, eventually leading to his return to work.

But the reality soon dawned on us. David would require practically round-the-clock care. At first, it seemed reasonable in the circumstances. He had been through so much over the past few months, not least surgery, and this sudden change of scene would no doubt require a few tweaks to our daily routine that could be incorporated gradually.

But it was not turning out like that. To say caring for my 22-year-old son was like looking after a baby would be no exaggeration. I probably do not need to go into too many details, but apart from the crying, everything else was similar to how it had been two decades earlier. Talking to him was not far from talking to a pre-school toddler; he could not comprehend simple sentences and attempts to construct one himself resulted in a jumbled, garbled and barely intelligible stream of vowels and consonants. What was different was the fact that babies can be picked up, moved around, cleaned, dressed and fed with relative ease, despite the inevitable wriggling and tantrum throwing, because they are feeble and light. David was a fully grown man with the weight and strength that made his unwillingness to do what was required an insurmountable obstacle.

He had also begun to retreat within himself, unable or unwilling to show emotions and expressing apathy to all but the cravings of his stomach and bladder. Time had become a meaningless concept to David. There was no such thing as day or night, let alone meal times or the other daily routines of those caring for him.

All this soon became mentally, physically and emotionally draining for everyone, especially me, and all that sustained me was the knowledge that in a week or two his needs would start to abate and that he would be able to start taking on more personal tasks himself, leading to the point when he would eventually be self-sufficient. Once this started to look unlikely, it became difficult to put his recovery into any sort of perspective. I was also feeling that I was neglecting his brother John somewhat, and like any 11-year-old he did not complain, preferring to keep things to himself, fully understanding that the situation was bigger than any of the seemingly trivial things that might have been worrying him. And yes, I guiltily allowed myself to admit that perhaps I had not been allowed to spend time on myself, on little treats, relaxation, putting things to the back of my mind for a moment and having some time to myself. Looking back, and observing others in the same position, it's not at all unreasonable. After all, the carer is the gatekeeper to the patient's rehabilitation, so their welfares are inextricably linked. But when it is you – and your son – it is difficult to be calculated and rational. So guilt was beginning to nibble at me, and there was nothing I could do about it.

I was looking forward to the postoperative appointment on 16 October. I would be able to tell the consultant what had been happening and hopefully get some assistance or at least advice. I felt that things were not right and that the doctor would straight away recognise this. After a greater than normal struggle to prepare David for the journey, we arrived at the surgery and I started to let off steam, Mr Winner feigning concern while I talked about a typical day in our household and he scribbled notes and filled forms. When I finished I sat back and awaited some life-improving statement from the consultant.

"Well, the good news," he began, "is that it appears that David is well on the path to recovery, and I shall be happy to recommend his returning to work in November."

My jaw dropped. "Have you listened to what I just said?" I gasped. He seemed to have ignored everything, from the slurring to the incontinence, and had somehow concluded that this man was fit enough to operate a fork-lift truck, when in fact he was barely able to operate a fork.

His face reddened and he raised his voice aggressively. "Who are you to question me, a consultant neurosurgeon?" he boomed with all the pomposity of a fairytale emperor. "I am very busy. Get out."

I was in tears, yet he offered me nothing in the way of reassurance, let alone apology. He repeated his dismissal.

The following week I went to see the family's GP to voice my concerns and get a second opinion. But he more or less went along with Mr Winner's line, saying that he was in no position to go over the head of a consultant neurosurgeon. At the time, before I had educated myself in the law of healthcare, I had no idea that everyone is entitled to a second opinion, but like most people I took the doctor at his word and shrugged in concurrence. After much persuading, he did agree to write out a sick note, which would at least keep the mortgage lender off David's back for a little longer, but he was falling behind with his payments, and this was another worry; if he had been deemed well enough to work, he would probably have lost his home.

The headaches got no better as November ground on. Although they were not constant, they seemed to hit him sharply, as though something was triggering them; but what this was, nobody could say. I would visit the GP weekly, each visit raising my concerns and hoping that the mere duration of the sickness and the lack of any sign of improvement would eventually force some kind of response, but I received no further assistance; only sympathetic words.

The last person I wanted to see was Mr Winner, but as far as I could make out he was the only person with the administrative power to get things moving. I booked an appointment for 17 December. He made no pretence that he was pleased to see me, and absent-mindedly endured my report about David's condition and my concerns that something as yet undetected had been impeding his recovery. When I reached the part where I told him that David was not yet back at work, he stopped me, and with incredulity in his voice said that this was totally unacceptable, and that there was no reason why he should not work. In fact, this seemed to be his sole concern. It was as though David's return to work would signal the end of his involvement, a signing-off if you like, a bureaucratic and unconcerned response if ever there was one. He went on to tell me that I was an overwrought and overprotective mother, and that David would never recover until he was forced to start looking after himself. Then he told me that it could in fact be me who was in need of professional help, and that I should see my GP about myself, not my son. Medication was recommended. As the tears of despair flowed ever more readily from my eyes, not a shred of empathy assaulted his toughened, uncaring intellect. In fact, it made him even more belligerent, and he ended our meeting by bellowing "Get a life!", marching to the door, yanking it open and screaming "Now get out!" I vividly recall the faces of the other patients in the waiting room, pictures of horror piled onto their existing trepidation. I tried to explain that he had hit the nail on head, that there was no chance of my having a life while David was in this state, but my entreaty fell on deaf ears.

Back to my GP I went, but he had by now been briefed, and his instructions had been forced into line by Mr Winner. Apparently, David was indeed healthy enough to restart work, and there was no justification for continued sick leave. He allowed a further two weeks' sick leave, but after that, he said, there was nothing he could do.

My only hope now lay in the hands of David's employers. Perhaps because they had actually seen him attempting to work after the initial haemorrhage, they were sympathetic. They assured me that if there was any way in which they could help, they would.

David went back to work on 21 January. It was clear from the start that he would not be able to continue where he had left off before the holiday, so his employers put him on light duties. However, even this proved far more than he could cope with. They attempted to allocate the lightest, simplest tasks to him, but he was utterly incapable of doing even these. He simply could not understand instructions, and even though he knew the building like the back of his hand he would frequently get lost between rooms and forget what he had been asked to do. His movement was slow and halting, and before long he was not even asked to do anything and his colleagues started doing his jobs for him. He was effectively being paid just to turn up, with the full compliance of his colleagues and superiors, simply so that he could maintain an income and pay off his mortgage. It was lucky that he had been popular. Every morning I would dress my son, feed him his breakfast and then take him off to work where his colleagues would take the baton and then eventually he would be passed back to me to continue the care. He rarely completed a day. And yet nobody from within the medical establishment saw his case as worthy of assistance.

I continued to waste my time seeking help from my GP and from Mr Winner, but they were still singing from the same song sheet and progress was nonexistent. In April I even took David to the A&E department of Victoria General Hospital, hoping that he would be given a scan that would reveal what was preventing him from recovering, but after a three-hour wait he was given treatment for flu. This devastated me; it had been a struggle to get him to hospital, and then to endure the uncomfortable waiting room when all he wanted to do was lie down had been extremely distressing for both of us.

I tried the A&E tactic once again a few weeks later. David's headaches persisted, and dizziness, fatigue and a lack of sensation down the left side of his body were his constant companions. I thought it reasonable that if I kept trying, one day I would be allocated someone who might have a clue what could be wrong with David. This time a Dr Fisher was our contact, and as soon as he saw David's case notes he concluded that no examination was necessary; in other words, thou shalt not question the word of Mr Winner. He suggested a trip to our GP and sent us on our way. Another distressing, depressing, wasted day.

David would suffer blackouts or lose consciousness from time to time. His lethargy and apathy combined to create a person devoid of ambition or emotion, and without my constant assistance I doubt if he would ever have eaten or changed his clothes. He would sometimes wake in a confused and agitated state, stagger about and try to escape from the house. After one particularly bad episode on 1 October. I decided that he should not go back to work. He finished work a week later.

(As I write these dates down, I feel almost as though time has been compressed. Nearly two years have passed in the space of a page, as only 'notable' events are being related. Yet every day was full of an interminable routine punctuated by scares that were common enough not to need specifying, and all the time the torment of seeing my son going through hell was made bearable only by the notion that soon it would all be over.)

I took David to see Mr Winner at the end of October, when he reiterated his opinion that it was perhaps not David who needed help but I. He also told me, with a threatening tone, that some doctors might see my actions as evidence that I was an unfit mother, and that if I persisted, David might end up being taken into care. He urged me to seek psychological help. Despite the dreadful way in which Mr Winner treated me, I still held a modicum of respect for him. It is difficult to explain, but perhaps I felt an element of awe for the person who had, as I saw it, saved my son's life. Looking back it seems utterly irrational, but at the time I was not thinking rationally, although not in the sense that Mr Winner was suggesting. I think I might have seen him as the man who had the power of life or death over David. I felt that no matter how terrible the things he said to me, and his lack of action with regard to my son's state, I had to keep in his good books because he was the only barrier between life and death.

And I think he knew it.

I was sobbing in front of him, perhaps reinforcing the impression he had already built up. He then made firm what he had intimated before, and said that if ever I set foot in the hospital again, I would be sectioned and David would be put into care.

By November my trips to the GP had become a regular event. It was becoming part of my routine, driven on by a hope that one day someone would say something different from everyone else; see what was evidently the truth; listen to me; go against what everyone else was saying. On one occasion I requested an appointment with

Blind alleys **27**

a neurologist, only to be told that there was a four- to six-month waiting list, unless of course I was prepared to pay to go private. The idea of such a wait filled me with dread, and David was, I thought, deteriorating. I borrowed the money and an appointment miraculously became available the following week.

This time we saw Dr Yorath, a neurologist (whom I would months later meet again – on NHS duty), and on this occasion there was no referral letter so David's history was down to my description. I related the whole story, from the fall and the treatment abroad, through the diagnosis and medication, to the current picture, of a man losing his grip on life, incapable of remembering things that had happened moments earlier and forgetting how to perform ingrained tasks such as working a television remote control.

Dr Yorath asked what medication David was on in view of the fact that he was suffering dizziness and headaches. I told him that as soon as he was deemed fit enough to return to work, his medication had been stopped. Dr Yorath looked surprised. "No wonder David was suffering these symptoms," he said, "it would appear that David is suffering epileptic fits." He became quite agitated and asked why his medication had been stopped. I told him that it was on the instruction of the Victoria General Hospital, and he calmed down a little. He then said that he wanted David to have a brain scan and an ECG. These could be performed at the Victoria General Hospital in Prestwick, where he was based, and that from then on he would see David at the Whitely Hospital, where he had an office, as his patient. He requested that David's case notes be sent to him so that he could get up to speed on what had happened up until that point. He also said that David should only go back to work on light duties for the time being. I felt elated, for the first time in many months, as though at last something was starting to happen. He prescribed Epilim to prevent the seizures he believed were happening, but emphasised that it must be taken regularly to have the desired effect.

In January David had a brain scan at the Victoria General Hospital and it was discovered that there was loose blood in his brain, which was almost certainly behind the left-side episodes. Dr Yorath was alarmed that David had not been taking Epilim, and showed dismay that it had been the Victoria General that had instructed our local clinic to stop the prescription. He made sure we understood how important it was that he continued with it. He thought that David should have been on the drug for at least a year, and probably eighteen months, because of the two haemorrhages.

(Years later I was to find out that this had been due to an error. David had been taking warfarin to thin his blood and carbamazepine for the epilepsy, but when the instruction was sent through for him to stop using the warfarin, it was wrongly phrased "cease all medication". It was shocking to find out that the pain, peril and torment we, especially David, had all been put through was entirely avoidable. Even the traumatic visits to Mr Winner would probably have not been necessary. But perhaps more seriously, it was because of this error that David will have to be on medication for the rest of his life.)

In April the dosage of Epilim was increased, and Dr Yorath instructed that David should not be allowed to drive a car. This followed a hair-raising incident when David skidded and crashed while driving. He had had a blackout. Fortunately no one was hurt, but I always believed that David should not even have been behind the wheel. Yet my opinion counted for nothing compared to that of somebody in the Social Security who, probably more to keep unemployment figures down than considering road safety, saw no reason why David should not drive (and therefore do his job as a fork-lift truck driver). Anyone merely looking at David and seeing the way he moved, spoke and reacted would have known straight away that he was not fit to drive, but the combined forces of the medical establishment and the Social Security knew better. And this was despite the many tests, tribunals and examinations that had shown in no uncertain terms that something was amiss. I suppose I can hardly blame the DSS pen-pushers who are not medically trained and have to take a professional's word for it, despite what they see with their own eyes. It seemed that all roads led to Mr Winner, and then there was a dead end.

Blind alleys

As a last resort I visited Mr Winner and said that I accepted that David was going back to work but would like him to write a note for his insurers to attempt to get some money to help him out and possibly recoup some of the mounting debts I had built up. "Absolutely not," he replied. "David is fit for work. There is nothing wrong with him." To qualify, after all, David would have to have been permanently disabled or off work for a year or more, and because of his return to work, this would cancel out any chances. In other words, he missed out on potentially £20,000 because he was forced back to work when he was clearly in no position to do so. In contrast, Dr Yorath thought that David should have had a year off work, but as usual his word counted for nothing against that of the mighty Mr Winner.

However, my trust in Dr Yorath was to be tested to destruction. As I saw him more and more, and David's condition gradually got worse, he started to take the official line, which was that there appeared to be nothing wrong. I started to get the impression that he had stopped listening to a word I said, and moreover had stopped caring. In many ways his manner and attitude began to resemble those of Mr Winner, and I started dreading my visits to a doctor I had once seen as David's potential life-saver. After one meeting, he brought up some detail that was clearly not true, and it took me by surprise. Suspicion crept up on me; I asked if he had read David's file, and was horrified when he told me that it had been mislaid. He tried to tell me that this was fine as long as David continued with his medication, and his offer of words of reassurance were less than welcome: "It happens all the time; don't worry." At this, I snapped back that something was not right here. But once again I had committed the mortal sin of questioning the word of a doctor. Only this time my justification was unquestionable. In medical matters I was not the expert. I'll grant Mr Winner that for the sake of argument. But losing a person's medical file? Surely that can't ever be right. But apparently not. Something that could result in a sacking down at the golf club was par for the course in a clinic.

Then out rolled the Winner speciality. It was not David who needed help; it was I. Perhaps I should go and see my GP and ask that I be put on medication. This, it was beginning to appear, was the standard response to anyone who suggested that their doctor was anything less than omniscient.

It was much later that my bemusement at Dr Yorath's change of attitude explained itself. I happened to find out that he and Mr Winner were actually close friends. When I first met Dr Yorath, perhaps they had not compared notes, or perhaps my private status obliged him to take the caring tone. Or maybe Mr Winner knew he had made mistakes and Dr Yorath was conveniently placed to perform a litigation-free cover-up. But how could I know the answer? I am disturbed, don't forget.

When I visited my GP, Dr Barrat, and filled him in with all the latest developments, he (as expected) told me that his hands were tied as he was not a specialist. At least he could see that David was not fit for work, however. His response was to keep feeding me with sick notes, each time for some slightly different ailment than the last, sometimes real, other times fictitious, as the genuine illness could not be used as the official specialist denial of it was legally binding. "You just have to know how to play the game," he would say. But consecutive mix and match maladies would never qualify David for any kind of disability pay, so financially we continued to struggle.

Time after time over the years of illness I would try and claim benefits for David. I was invariably rebuffed, because David was not ill; he was lazy, apparently. The fall in the shower, the brain haemorrhage, the operations, the blackouts, the loss of memory and the epilepsy were just one big coincidence, and had nothing whatsoever to do with David's ability to work. He was just workshy. If they told me this enough times, would I start to believe it? He could claim unemployment benefit and that was it. But continued eligibility was dependent upon his applying for three jobs a week. I would say that he could walk back into his old job tomorrow if he suddenly got better, but he is unable to work. So they would stop the benefit. I would contest the decision. The benefit would start again. This happened countless times. It was little more than a game to them. At times I would be passed around from department to department, sometimes moving sideways, sometimes up the echelons, usually down, but all the time wasting hours of my life when I could have been earning a living myself or caring for David. I once reached someone in the government, but was told that I had to follow the correct procedure like everyone else.

These people had a way of making my suggested mental problems a self-fulfilling prophecy. Every so often I would read a newspaper and see an exposé of someone who had been caught running a marathon or working as a builder while claiming incapacity benefits. How come they could manage this whereas I could not help my son when his problems were impossible to miss? I was certainly being tested. But something inside me kept me going.

Another glimmer of hope flickered to life. I noticed a leaflet in my GP's surgery about a charity called Headline for head injury victims. I had never heard of them before, and not a single person in any of the hospitals or clinics I had visited had ever pointed out its existence. I immediately rang the number, and made an appointment with a Mr Allen, a volunteer who worked from the Victoria General Hospital. We met a few days later. Mr Allen struck me as the most genuine person I had dealt with to date. It turned out that his inspiration to volunteer was not far removed from the situation I was in; his son had suffered a brain injury and had survived but was paralysed. His sympathy for my plight was evident. He said that before we could progress he would need David's case notes, and since this could not be done instantly (of course, this would have been utterly beyond the scope of human endeavour), we would have to make a second appointment.

A few days later we returned as planned. David's case notes could not be located. Nor could Mr Allen's caring attitude. Like so many before him, Mr Allen's helpful tone had evaporated after a promising start. He spent more time trying to bring my attention to the fact that David smoked than to his serious medical condition. He also started off on the usual 'get back to work' spiel. We sat through all this, sinking into despair. He indicated that David's condition had bottomed out and that he could not get any worse, suggesting that from now on, the only way was up. Yet with every passing day I was observing his decline in measurable ways.

He then concluded the meeting by telling us that there was no point in us ever seeing him again. What a charitable chap!

After such palpable optimism, the fall was painful. Whenever I thought I was emotionally drained, some plug would be pulled and I would realise that I had in fact been swimming in hitherto unknown reserves; surely I was now down to my last drops.

This is not the best state to be in if you're planning some serious detective work, but the obvious truth dawned on me one night. A pattern had emerged. People would see David and me; they would start off optimistic; they would lose case notes; they would suddenly turn truculent and aggressive; they would work at the same hospital. Something was going on. People were closing ranks.

Out of desperation I made another private appointment with Dr Yorath. On my arrival I was greeted with a red-faced "What are you doing here?" I explained that I needed more help and that it only seemed forthcoming when I paid for it myself. The NHS line was that he was fine and needed no therapy and that none was available anyway. As soon as I explained that the tingling and headaches had abated since medication started but that his memory loss was at an unmanageable level, he decided once again that this did not preclude him from returning to work as long as he was put on light duties. "In fact," he went on, "this is probably just what he needs." He actually phoned David's place of work to arrange for him to resume his employment, but on that occasion there was nobody about who could deal with the instruction. The appointment ended in the usual manner, with Dr Yorath getting angry and telling me not to come back, and suggesting once again that I should see my GP about my own health, and start by asking for some sleeping tablets. The last thing I wanted was to be knocked unconscious every night. I would practically sleep with one eye open and I'm sure that this approach had in the past saved David from serious injury on more than one occasion.

Days later, Dr Yorath's bill for £100 dropped through my letterbox. I was aghast at the audacity – he had made no attempt to help David. In a fit of spontaneous rage I ripped the bill up and phoned him up to tell him not to expect a penny from me. Of course, I got through to

Blind alleys **33**

his blameless secretary and had to tone down my anger somewhat. "I'll ... I'll speak to Dr Yorath about it, but he won't be happy," she muttered. I told her to remind him that he had not helped my son whatsoever and ended up ejecting me from his office, and that even if he threatened to take me to court I would not be paying him. It crossed my mind that maybe the legal profession were in cahoots with the medical profession, but I took my chance.

And still, weeks later, I found myself making more appointments with him. No matter where I looked, no matter how much help I tried to find from all manner of places, every door seemed to be slammed in my face. It felt as though he had somehow made himself my only port of call, because whoever I spoke to looking for help would always seem promising at first but eventually inform me that without official word from David's specialist, nothing could be done. And finding another specialist was all but impossible. So with my tail between my legs but a fight in my heart I would make the journey to his office, watch him roll his eyes on my arrival, hear the same old story and endure his closed mind once again. I guess I was continually hoping that some revolutionary head injury treatment had the previous week been discovered, and that one week I would show up and be greeted by Dr Yorath with a smile, a handshake and the words, "I've been waiting to see you. I have the most fantastic news ..." But what I got was "No treatment needed. None available. *Next.*"

That is until one week, when he improvised the script to satisfy his perceptions of me. He said "None needed. And in any case, you couldn't afford it anyway." I stood and stared at him (having long since stopped bothering to sit down). My jaw dropped involuntarily as I took in the implications of what he had just said. Surely it had just slipped out, or perhaps he was so frustrated with me that he wanted to ratchet up the power game a degree, because as I heard it, he had just admitted that treatment was, and had been, available all this time – but not on the NHS. Through all my tears, pleading, arguments, tests, tortuous visits and futility, he had smugly sat there shaking his head, passing many chances to mention it to me so that perhaps *I* could have decided whether or not I could have afforded it.

I decided there and then that there was no going back to Dr Yorath after this. He seemed to be willingly negligent and quite possibly the most arrogant person I had ever met. And yet, as I strode out of his surgery, anger was the furthest thing from my mind, as, for the first time since this whole nightmare began, I had heard that there existed a potentially expensive but life-changing treatment, and I was topped up with the vigour that had been drained out of me over the months of sleepless nights and long, helpless, depressing days.

4

Struggle, hardship and a new hope

With renewed optimism I recalled the events that had assaulted me over the previous years from a different perspective. . The years seemed to form blocks of time that could be ordered as distinct phases in David's decline and improvement. First there was the year of the accident, when 24-hour care and a virtual return to a state of infancy had been the only way to keep my son alive.

Dreadful headaches were the theme of the next year, when David was also frustrated and occasionally hurt by the then inexplicable tingling that continued up and down his left side, sometimes arriving with a terrifying, disorienting suddenness that would make him shout out and, depending on the time of day, have me drop everything or fumble around in the dark to be by his side.

Then the tingling had been discovered to be a symptom of epilepsy and largely brought under control by daily medication. But the tingling was replaced by a weakness down his left side, which precluded him from going back to his old job properly, and caused strange muscular phenomena like his inability to release something that he had picked up; I lost count of the number of times I had to prise the television remote control from his hand, long after he had forgotten what he had wanted to turn up, down or over, or sometimes what this strange lump of plastic in his hand actually did. The inability to loosen his grip applied to toilet roll, too. When visiting the toilet he could not let go of it, and would end up flushing whole unravelled rolls down the lavatory – or at least trying to, with predictable results. Yet compared to everything else going on, a bit of amateur plumbing seemed quite trivial, and once he had explained that he was powerless to let go of the roll, we both actually found this amusing every time it happened, even though it was disturbing (I think it's called toilet humour).

The toilet roll problem did occur during his short stint at work, to the point where staff would complain that someone was trying to cause trouble by blocking the toilets. One colleague told David that he was going to find out who was doing it and report them, and asked for his help in finding out who was the last visitor next time it happened. On one occasion this self-appointed U-bend vigilante emerged from the cubicle shouting, "The bastard! They've done it again! I was only distracted for a minute and they went and did it!" David kept his mouth shut, partly through a desire not to get caught, but mainly through embarrassment.

The grip problem also occurred when David shook hands with anyone. Although it was a serious problem, somehow it seemed to provide light relief, partly because of the puzzled looks that would appear on people's faces as they tried to work out whether such a long handshake was ever going to end. At first I had to physically straighten his fingers, but in time he learnt to do it with his other hand.

With the weakness, David was also excluded from his second love after football – cooking. Although he tried and tried, it was out of the question. Trying to handle knives and hot pans was far too dangerous, and before he resigned himself to eating other people's culinary attempts, he managed to scald himself a few times. The kitchen was the location for a real near miss caused by a combination of lack of memory and weakness. One night when I was fast asleep, David got up to cook something, but either forgot how or lacked the strength to cause a spark to ignite the hob. Instead of turning off the gas, he merely went back to bed. I awoke to the smell of gas and fortunately recalled those TV public information films where the man shouts "Stop!" at the woman about to turn on the light. Thankfully he had not had the urge to light a cigarette that night.

Another source of torment was David's dogged unwillingness to change his clothes, even his underwear. He would wear the same outfit day after day, and if I should suggest a change of clothes he would become uncharacteristically aggressive and tell me to mind my own business. I eventually found a way past this particular issue. Like some

Struggle, hardship and a new hope **37**

distracted tooth fairy, I would creep into his room while he slept and replace his pile of discarded clothes with an equally strewn – yet clean – outfit and put the old ones in the wash. As far as he was concerned, he was winning this battle and never changing; and although this was purely down to his dreadful memory, it was a relief to have a solution.

Every morning, I would shout and scream at him to get out of bed, an act he resisted as determinedly as he did changing clothes. When he finally did get up and put on his clothes, he would merely place himself in a chair facing the TV, regardless of whether it was turned on or not. I had to tell him to eat, to drink and to go to the toilet, and although it hurt to have to do this, he would otherwise just sit there all day and occasionally soil himself. He would stare at me in a defensive, childish way, full of resentment towards me for trying to move him from his state, and giving the impression that he would much rather I was not there. This aggression would occasionally spill over to affect his little brother, in whose eyes David had changed from someone he idolised into someone he feared.

Nothing could stop the headaches that were painful enough to observe, let alone endure at first hand. Just a loud noise could trigger another hour or two of this agony, as could all manner of unpredictable experiences, which meant that whenever possible David had to be closeted away and insulated from all potential external shocks, and spend whole days just lying down in bed.

The loss of memory always seemed to take second place to the more physical symptoms in the eyes of the medical authorities, so it was never given much attention, and was never really seen as particularly noteworthy in itself, yet it made my son into a person lacking confidence and unable to function in society. Thanks to a lack of financial support, he had little choice but to continue being part of society that would occasionally take advantage of his timidity and trusting nature.

But slowly, by sticking to a routine, David started to come out of himself. He needed to be kept occupied and change had to be managed gradually, on a weekly or monthly basis; but with patience from all around him, he started to show signs of becoming stronger.

Looking at the calendar and seeing that this phase had lasted for

38   *Return from Nowhere*

some two years caused a jolt of shock. At times it felt as though nothing much had happened, such was the slowness of his recovery.

But now, all of a sudden, it looked as if Dr Yorath had let slip that a treatment was available – at a cost, and I dared to imagine that in a few months' time the whole family might have taken a giant step back towards normality.

Daily life at that time was almost always an immense struggle, but every now and again something would happen that could raise a smile through the torment.

Take, for example, the occasion when I had decided to pop out to the shops while David slept one afternoon. I never normally left him for more than a few seconds, but after checking that he seemed fine and safe in the knowledge that my trip would take no more than half an hour, I set out. Waking David up and going through the rigmarole of shepherding him through the town when the slightest distraction could have him wandering off when my back was turned did not seem like an easy option.

I did my shop and as I walked through my door I could hear voices, one of which was definitely David's, coming from the kitchen. The sight that confronted me will remain in my head forever. My son was accompanied by three jovial tramps, who wore the standard tramp garb that was the stuff of cliché, right down to dirty, straggly hair and a rope in lieu of a belt. They all seemed pleased to see me. I was too shocked to be angry, and turned away from and covered my face as I tried desperately to stifle a guffaw. What followed hardly helped keep my face straight.

"These," David announced, "are old school friends of mine." Although it is difficult to age swarthy, dirty skin, one thing was clear – these men were at least twice David's age. "They've fallen on hard times."

"Is that so?" I said.

"Yes," he continued. "And I said you'd cook them a meal."

"That was very nice of you, David."

One of the vagrants then piped up "I mean, we don't want it for nothing. We'll do some work for you. We can dig the garden or fit new handles on the doors." I thought this was a strange odd-job to offer, and it must have shown on my face, because he then pointed at me in a 'watch this' kind of way and undid his rope and, in the manner of a flasher or a wartime spiv, opened up his overcoat to reveal an array of door handles in every imaginable style and state of repair.

I scanned the collection of handles and quickly realised that no two were the same. I was assuming these weren't samples of the ones he would order from the warehouse. "They're no good," I said, shaking my head. "None of them match the ones in the house – in fact, none of them match each other!"

"Well," he sighed, "it's hard to get complete sets nowadays. The pub landlords know to keep an eye on us!"

"Sorry," I concluded. "I'm happy with the handles I've got. And you can't dig over my garden because I don't have a spade."

"Oh," the same man, clearly the ringleader, interjected. "That's not a problem. Just give us five minutes and we'll be back with a spade." They shuffled as if to leave. Tempted as I was to let the three of them and their pervading stink roll out of the house so I could bolt them out, the idea of them breaking into a neighbour's garden shed and emerging with a spade made me stop them.

"No," I said. "And anyway, I couldn't afford to pay you." This was not far from the truth. "I'll make you a sandwich and a drink, and then you'll have to go." They looked at each other, smiling and shaking their heads as if to say that I was obviously mistaken, then prompted David to clear up the matter.

"Oh, I said they could stay the night," David explained, nonchalantly.

For a moment I was dumbfounded. "Impossible!" I whined, exasperation beginning to show. "There's no room here."

"Oh. We've thought about that," said David in his most reassuring tone. "Two of them will have my bedroom and I'll sleep downstairs with the other.

I made them their sandwiches and gave them a drink, all of which they consumed heartily. I realised that they did not exactly look underfed. They may have been tramps but there was nothing wrong with their canny powers of manipulation, which is probably a vital survival tool on the lawless streets. When one of them used the toilet, I had to go in after him to make sure he had not relieved me of my lock or door handle. My protection sandwich must have done the trick as he left them intact. I then gave them the last five pound note I had and sent them on their way. Just as we were seeing them out, one of the neighbours was arriving home, and he saw David shouting "See you, mate" to them as they left. I shall never forget the look on his face.

Back in the house the inquisition began. It turned out David had met them at the bookmaker's, which was, I realised, further from the house than were the shops I had been to. David could obviously be quite nimble when he wanted to be. I resolved to keep an even closer eye on him in future.

Although the tramp episode was as strangely light and amusing then as it is to recount, it was further evidence of the fact that David's mind was not working as it should have been. On the one hand he was withdrawn and often truculent; on the other he was vulnerable, trusting, convivial and lacking social inhibitions.

Because of the expenses that were mounting up, I eventually had to sell my car to raise a bit of money. I was therefore pleased when a friend of mine let me borrow his car when he went on holiday. But even this turned into a headache one evening when David had one of his tantrums and stormed upstairs, audibly slamming his door, ostensibly behind him. In fact, he had then taken the car keys and crept out of the house to go for a drive, a fact that was not revealed to me until I popped my head around his door before going to bed. This put me in an inescapable dilemma. If I rang the police, we could all have got into trouble as David's epilepsy precluded him from driving, and the thought of any brushes with the law reminded me of Mr Winner's threat that David could be taken into care if I was seen as being unfit to look after him. At the same time, doing nothing could have been dangerous, as David was clearly unfit to drive, and threatened himself and others with injury every second he spent at the wheel. All I could think of doing was ringing round all of my family members and David's friends, asking if they had seen him. I was virtually spooning dry instant coffee into my mouth in an attempt to stay awake, until fatigue eventually got the better of me and I drifted off.

Struggle, hardship and a new hope   **41**

I woke with a jolt at seven the next morning and checked to see if the car was there. My heart stopped when I saw that it was not, and worse, David was not in the house. Moments later though, I heard the engine cut off outside as David parked, walked into the house and headed straight for his room as though nothing had happened. He went to sleep and I left him to it as I leapt outside to check the car for scratches, dents and mangled limbs. Fortunately all seemed well. He slept for the rest of the day and when he eventually emerged I exploded trying to get through to him how dangerous his actions had been. He seemed quite unperturbed by my rant and took a leaf from the doctors' books, calmly suggesting that I seek psychological assistance.

We would later find out that David's behaviour and his general functioning were all typical effects of frontal lobe damage. This part of the brain has many functions, among which are judgement, the application of social skills, control and movement. However, David's intelligence was in many ways intact, as was evidenced by the deviousness he could call upon when he wanted something he felt was being kept from him. Both my father's and my own credit cards fell into his clutches, and he even sold his own jewellery, took cash, and anything else that he thought had value, almost invariably to get money with which to gamble. And the way he could manipulate people (despite being the victim of others' schemes) required an advanced awareness of people's personalities.

So from then on I had to hide the car keys, along with the money and credit cards, as seeing either would give him a one-track mind that led directly to the bookie's. I do not really believe he thought of it as stealing, and I'm pretty sure he had no concept of the financial trouble we were in, so I found it hard to blame him too much. Still, it was difficult to live with someone who did not understand the concept of sharing, who thought that everything in the house was his to steal, sell or destroy, and who begrudged his mother or brother having anything to call their own.

David's attitude towards his brother was equally worrying. He would start verbally abusing him the moment he got home from school, and his aggressive outbursts, coupled with his lack of sensitivity towards others, were frightening and often extremely hurtful. Before long it started to affect John and his school work, so he started sleeping over at friends' houses a few nights a week. It was always difficult to judge how everything was affecting John, who seemed so strong. He remembered the old, easy-going David who was a friend, a brother and an avuncular figure all rolled into one, and like all of us wanted him back. John was probably too young to appreciate that David's behaviour was not directed at him personally, but was illustrative of his unwillingness to share anything – in this case my attention. Although an outsider might have thought that David hated me, in reality he relied on me for everything (whether given or stolen), and saw my offering time and affection to John as some kind of betrayal. If he had planned to get John out of the scene, he succeeded.

I took all these stories to Dr Yorath in an attempt to describe a personality that was clearly not fully functional, indeed dangerous. But of course there was 'nothing wrong' – unless I could afford to pay for treatment.

* * *

During the weekend of Dr Yorath's gasp-inducing declaration that treatment could be offered if I could afford it, my mother was watching a TV programme called *Link*, which that week happened to be about head and brain injuries. She took down the helpline number, which promised to help make contact with specialists. After all the disappointments and blind alleys I was reluctant to call, but my mother persuaded me that there was really nothing to lose, and I eventually agreed with her and gave it a try. The fact that I now saw a glimmer of hope probably won it for me; but this was a completely new contact and I was wary. I made the phone call, and a few days later I received leaflets and advice about centres where help for head injuries could be sought. One in particular stood out due to its closeness: the The Meadows in Castleton. My contact there was a Dr Richard Bond, and when I phoned him and explained the situation, he immediately seemed positive that something could be done. He expressed surprise that things had been dragging on for so long because he was certain that treatment was, and had for some time been, available.

Dr Bond was probably the first person I ever spoke to who seemed

Struggle, hardship and a new hope **43**

to be genuinely concerned, and listened patiently when I spoke; this all heartened me immensely. Surely finding someone with a truly caring attitude would help David. He was concerned that so little had been done during the crucial first twelve months of David's injury – and, indeed, thereafter – as every week that passes without treatment chips away at the chances of a full recovery.

At last Dr Bond said he thought he should see us both as soon as possible. I was ecstatic. Two options were presented: that we could go to Castleton or he would visit us. I explained our financial situation and told him we had sold the car. He thought for a moment then said that he would visit us, and waive the £200 fee for the two-hour initial assessment by himself and the physiotherapist. My confidence in Dr Bond was growing by the second, and I bombarded him with questions which, to his credit, he answered in the same measured way to which I had quickly become accustomed. An urgent appointment was arranged.

I cannot describe how high I was that evening. Through all the tribulations I had never given up hope, despite the feeling of being closed in by everyone who had the potential to help. Yet this time I sensed a real opening, a cool blast of fresh air that filled me with a renewed determination to press forward. All it had taken was a phone call; a few encouraging words; an intimation that despite what everyone else seemed to be saying, it was not I who had the problem, it was David. Because after a while, after being ground down so that your rough edges of resistance have been smoothed like those of pebbles in a stream, it is possible to start thinking how much easier life could be if you just accepted what they said and gave up the struggle. Perhaps I was close to this point; I will never know. But now, I felt my life flowing back. Roll on the examination.

At the end of May, the doctor and the physiotherapist made their visit. He more or less reiterated what he had said on the phone, that urgent treatment should be sought and that he could not believe how ineffectual the treatment so far had been. He was sure that, with the correct care in the immediate aftermath of the injury, David's life could well have been back to normal by now, even to the point of playing football again. This was not exactly what I had wanted to hear, partly because I already knew it, and partly because it was irrelevant to the situation we faced. Instead I needed some results.

The way forward would be an intensive rehabilitation programme. Because of all that had preceded the current situation, there was little chance of getting this paid for by the NHS, so the only route open was private. Although the thought had horrified me in the past, it seemed that the only option would be to sell David's house to pay for it. I had practically no assets left, and although my parents' financial help had been nothing short of life-saving, I could not rely on it for ever.

I asked Dr Bond if treatment could start straight away if I went to the estate agent's that afternoon and put his house on the market. He seemed unsure about this, partly because the initial funds would need to be in place beforehand, and partly because the entire programme would need to be completed for the treatment to be effective; indeed, stopping it halfway through if we ran out of money would be both a waste of money and potentially distressing for David. I started to tot up in my head how long it would take to release the value of David's home; it would be a minimum of several weeks, and that would probably be if we did not ask for the full value of the home. Still, an injection of the £20,000 I estimated the sale would raise would no doubt help in the long term.

Although I would have liked to get going immediately, I realised we would have to wait another month or so, and calmly asked Dr Bond about what private treatment would cost.

"Well," he began, "the programme will take eighteen months from start to finish, but for full therapeutic treatment two years is preferable. The costs will be £1,500 per week."

Everything around me crumbled to dust. The enthusiasm, the optimism, the trust and the determination that had been fortifying me over the previous days were swept away with a simple bit of mental arithmetic. Even if I sold David's house, the funds it would release would pay for about three months of a two-year programme. My open mouth dried up and I stood staring at the face whose mouth had just delivered such a crushing sentence.

I sensed that he already knew it would be out of our reach financially.

Struggle, hardship and a new hope **45**

I shook my head and started mentally to wrap up the assessment, which was beginning to seem pointless. I asked if there was even the slightest chance that this could be done on the NHS. Surprisingly, he seemed quite optimistic, and cited cases of people having similar treatment paid for, some of which were actually at his own unit.

Dr Bond advised me to go to my GP with this development, and to tell him that David had undergone this assessment and that my GP should authorise payment by Social Services for treatment. It was a stark reminder of who remained the gatekeeper to David's fate, and once again the rollercoaster took a heart-stopping plunge.

He then said something strange: he asked me not to mention his name at all with respect to the examination, and told me that his findings and prognosis letter would be anonymous. Politics was evidently rearing its head again, but whatever Dr Bond's reasons, I resolved to follow his advice. He did warn me that it would not be easy, that the medics and their administrators would continuously throw obstacles in our path, but that if I stuck to my guns and persevered, the funds would eventually be released. Most of this was not new to me. We had run over the allotted two hours of the visit, in fact the fourth hour was nearly upon us, so I insisted that the doctor and the physiotherapist should get off to their next appointment. I thanked them profusely for coming, for waiving their fee and for showing such compassion and understanding, but mainly for giving me the advice, even if it would prove to be just another twinkle of hope that would fade away.

Before they left, they invited me to pay a visit to the unit to see for myself the excellent progress they had been making. I said I would love to. They explained that every case was treated differently, and that the patients were all regaining independence.

The following week my sister drove David and me there, and I was thoroughly reassured. The place certainly had 'private healthcare' written all over it. It was situated in a semi-rural location, with plenty of greenery, scenic views (the environs of Castleton are rolling and beautiful) and a relaxed atmosphere. All was calm, and the building and its decoration were well kept. Part of the process of rehabilitation is the induction of calmness and tranquillity, of creating routine and minimising the frequency and intensity of stressful events, so all this seemed logical and comforting. I was impressed with the level of security in place, too. I knew how easily David could slip past your watchfulness and wander away, sometimes aimlessly, sometimes with a navigator's acuity, but at least here I was convinced that he would get no further than the gates. I learnt about the 24-hour observation and the locked doors, and met staff and patients, all of whom struck me with their happiness and easy-going nature. David got on easily with his potential friends and the staff members, yet another factor in my growing respect for the establishment.

I dared to believe that this modest little place on the outskirts of Castleton could be where David could progress effectively; and even that I might be able to claw back a life of my own. It did not feel like a hospital, and I could picture myself sleeping soundly at night knowing that David was being cared for. There was also a twinge of anger that the establishment's existence had been kept from me by everyone I had so far encountered. No doubt the cost affected their decision, and that hurt.

Dr Bond approached me and handed me a letter. In it, he and his partner Margaret Beatty stated that they would be able to rehabilitate David for £1,500 a week for a minimum of eighteen months, with a further six-month stay an option if deemed necessary and agreed upon. I was to hand this letter to my GP as discussed at my house.

David did not want to leave. He seemed so happy and relaxed – in total contrast to the chaos that would roar back into our lives when we walked through my front door.

The very next morning I was sitting opposite Dr Barrat in his surgery and handing him the letter. He appeared indifferent to it, but commented that I looked better. I told him it could well have been a result of my new-found optimism, the source of which was manifested in the letter in his hands. He read through the notes in a cursory way, and as he reached the end, where I expected to see delight I read nothing in his face. He seemed awkward and standoffish, shuffling the papers about in his hands. I asked for some sort of reaction, but he looked blankly back at me.

"Where did you hear about this place?" he asked. I recalled Dr

Struggle, hardship and a new hope

Bond's request that he should not be identified, and told him that it had come up in a conversation with friends. He then went on with what I, and indeed Dr Bond, had predicted. There was no funding for such programmes on the NHS, and he certainly would not be authorising Social Services to provide it. I was, he said, welcome to contact them myself, but he intimated that I would be wasting my time.

Ignoring my GP's instincts – and to some extent my own – I wrote to Social Services and requested a visit by a social worker. This much was a success, but after his visit the social worker told me that he was sympathetic to David's plight but that no funding would be made available to send him to the rehabilitation unit. He did make two suggestions, both of which shook me. I could put David into a secure unit for a few weeks to allow me to have a holiday, or there was the possibility that he could get a place in a permanent secure lock-up, "so that he would not bother anyone ever again". Not for the first time in this saga, I was dumbfounded, but soon gathered my thoughts enough to tell the social worker that I actually *did* want David to bother someone, and that I wanted someone to be bothered about him in return. I had not expected this visit to result in what was tantamount to David's being thrown in prison.

The social worker continued his pretence of looking concerned, saying that he wished he could help but that there were people with much greater need who had been waiting much longer, so David stood very little chance of receiving treatment. He asked me not to take it personally. How else could I take it? He 'took sides' with me and said that if it were up to him, David would be in the rehab unit already, but that this was a political matter and that he was powerless. I started to wonder what the point of this man's job was. But really, it was obvious. In the grim calculations of healthcare, it is somehow more beneficial to pay for someone's lifelong minimal treatment than to fix them to become tax-paying, healthy citizens. It did not make any sense. I boiled up inside and threw the social worker out of the house, slamming the door on his offered apologies.

Back to square one? Not necessarily. I still had Dr Bond seemingly on my side. Surely he had dealt with similar cases, and from a purely financial point of view it would be in his interest to see to it that I could get funding.

I called him, and ended up having another strange conversation. It started normally enough; he expressed sympathy, told me not to give up and advised me to ask my GP for an assessment by the Consultant Physician in Rehabilitation Medicine, which would be on the NHS. I thanked him for his advice and said I would do as he said. "But as before," he added, "do not mention my name. If you do, and your GP gets in touch with me, I will deny ever having spoken to you. Is that clear?" It was a line straight out of a gangster movie or *Only Fools and Horses*, certainly not the type of thing you expect to hear from a professional. It was delivered even more forcefully than it had been when we first met, and it was disconcerting. But he knew how powerful he was, and that in my view he was the only option. So he would have known that seconds later I was agreeing with him, despite my misgivings. Perhaps it was something trivial – he could have trounced my GP on the squash court or slept with his wife or something. The chances are it was irrelevant to David's rehabilitation and none of my business. I had already learnt how diplomacy is more important than actual healthcare in the NHS.

I asked what would happen if Dr Barrat refused, and was told that legally, he could not refuse to send a letter to the consultant on David's behalf. "Of course," he warned, "getting a letter to the consultant and getting funding are two very different things. Even at best it can be a slow process. Just make sure your GP sends the letter and we can take it from there." He went on to say that the NHS outsources a lot of treatment to private health companies, but that they do not openly advertise the fact because of the costs involved, especially when it is borne in mind that my GP was a fundholder.

I went back to Dr Barrat and told him of this revelation and requested a letter of referral to the consultant, who turned out to be one Dr Kay Ingalls. Dr Barrat was dismayed to see me, as usual paying me little attention and avoiding eye contact. He told me that this was not something he could do straight away, but that I should make an appointment for another visit three days later. This I did, and when I

Struggle, hardship and a new hope   **49**

returned I was almost amused to see that Dr Barrat was not present, but a locum, Dr Khan, was in his seat. "How can I help you?" he asked.

"Oh, I've just come to pick up a letter of referral Dr Barrat has written for me."

"What letter?"

"It's a letter of referral to Dr Ingalls, Consultant Physician in Rehabilitation Medicine. Dr Barrat was writing it on behalf of my son. I am just here to pick it up."

"There is no letter," he said, looking me straight in the eye. "There must be some mistake."

"Yes, there must be. Dr Barrat told me to come back today. He has been writing it. He has obviously forgotten to mention it to you."

"No. He never mentioned a letter."

"Look in the drawer," I told him.

At this Dr Khan became quite irritated (as, it seems, doctors do when you suggest something to them). "Look," he almost shouted. "I would know if there was a letter in the drawer, and there is not. Perhaps Dr Barrat never intended to write you a letter of referral. You'll have to ask him yourself."

"When can I see him?"

"In five weeks. He's gone to India."

Until now I had assumed that my GP had fallen ill or was on urgent business, but his absence had clearly been arranged some time ago. No wonder he asked me to come back on this day. "I can't wait that long!" I exploded. "This is urgent."

Dr Khan shook his head and said, "Do you know how many hip replacements we could perform for the same cost as your son's rehabilitation? Forty. Did it ever cross your mind that the money could be better spent on other, more deserving, people?"

By the end of his speech I was in tears, sobbing to the doctor that I was not interested in how many hip operations could be done, and that if I was trying to jump the queue I must be the world's worst queue-jumper as I had waited four years so far. All I wanted was one letter. The consultant could even refuse to take it further, but that letter was the only thing preventing David from having a fair hearing.

Dr Khan passed me a tissue then asked me to leave. He was very busy, he told me.

"I will leave when I get the letter, Dr Khan," I said, with strength pulled from my reserves.

"Then I will call the police and have you removed."

"I have no life anyway," I said. "I don't care. Call them. Or write me the letter. It's up to you." He opened the hatch above his desk and called to his receptionist to call the police. "Call them," I repeated, "and I'll just tell them that you are ruining people's lives, that you are placing ridiculous obstructions in their paths." I saw the receptionist reaching for the phone and it dawned on me what would happen if the police did come, and if I were to spend the night in a cell. I shouted through to the receptionist not to call, and with tears rolling down my face I strode out of the surgery.

I was still highly distressed when I called Dr Bond once again, telling him what had happened. He said that my only hope now was to bypass my GP altogether and to write to Shipton Health Authority direct. Again there was his caveat – that I must not mention his name. He told me that he had already said a lot more than he should have. If this fails, please do not contact me again. I found this rather sinister. I could not understand why he needed to remain nameless, although a picture was forming in my mind of an NHS that was bound by the law but would go to great lengths to avoid it being exercised to its financial detriment. He wished us luck and hung up.

I got through to a Mr Malcolm at the Shipton Health Authority, and initially he took the same line as everyone else. He told me I had to go through my GP and that that was the only place from which a letter of referral would be accepted. Once again I broke down and started blurting out my story, right up until that day's events in the GP's surgery. I emphasised how critical the situation was and that a five-week wait for a letter – and then a wait of however long it took to process – was out of the question.

Mr Malcolm told me not to worry, and that he would write to Dr Ingalls himself. I asked him what I should do about the GP, and he told me not to worry about it. He said he would deal with this case

Struggle, hardship and a new hope

personally. It would still be going through my GP, but instead of being on my instruction it would be on his, so this was a whole new situation.

I believed and trusted Mr Malcolm, and gave him my sincerest thanks before bursting out crying again. He told me not to worry. In a few days the wheels would be in motion.

Relief and fatigue immediately swept over me. It was for the time being out of my hands, and it felt weird not knowing what to do next. I knew what I wanted to do and that was to sleep for a week, and I am sure I could have done.

But with my son to look after, this was just wishful thinking.

5

Concrete hopes

I finally met Dr Ingalls, the consultant, at the hospital, and she set about the long overdue assessment of David's condition. She told me what everyone except the medical decision-makers readily admitted – that David was suffering from weakness on his left side accompanied by pain, and that he had a residual cognitive deficit as a direct result of the haemorrhage. What was momentous about this conclusion was that until now assessors from numerous establishments had firmly stated that there was nothing wrong with him, – indeed that it was I who needed help.

I recall that when I recounted to Dr Ingalls several of the occasions when it had been denied that there was anything wrong with David, she slammed her hand angrily on the table at the injustice and incompetence. She even pointed out that she worked with Dr Yorath and that he knew about the work she did, and could not comprehend his decision not to at least refer David to her. She also denounced the claims by Social Services that funding would not be available, saying that David could even have been treated as an outpatient with their financing.

She was particularly disturbed by the length of time that had elapsed, as with head injuries the first twelve months are critical if rehabilitation is to succeed, and that after this length of time it becomes much more difficult to give the kind of vocational rehabilitation that completely reintegrates somebody into society. In David's current state and with passage of time, she warned, this could now take several years, and even then his employability was not guaranteed.

David's returning to employment at the behest of the doctors also dismayed her. She said that a minimum period of two years should

Concrete hopes **53**

ideally have passed between the accident and his returning to work, and even then it should have been following comprehensive rehabilitation. She seemed to agree that my GP had for some reason been putting obstacles between David and the treatment he so desperately needed.

Indeed, almost everything she said after this brief assessment tallied with what any casual observer would have noticed. Surely this would give my argument more weight, even though I had faith in Mr Malcolm's commitment.

With all that was going on, the chance for David to get some professional help was immeasurably welcome. I told Dr Ingalls about what my life had become since having to look after my son: how he gambled so much that I had ended up accompanying him to the bookies to keep an eye on him; how he would involuntarily swear at people and have no memory of it seconds later; how he would be over-affectionate with people, making him particularly attractive to homosexuals, who would often see it as a come-on. This last tendency also meant that I would have to occasionally take him into ladies' public toilets when we were out; I could not trust him on his own in gents'. This happened frequently, as his mind existed only in the present, and he would not have the foresight to go to the toilet before we went out. My continual care for him exceeded looking after his basic needs. I was actually required to be his conscience, to keep him out of trouble and to defuse potentially violent or plain awkward situations.

He also had no sense of self-preservation, evidenced by his regular dashes into the middle of busy roads, forcing cars to swerve to avoid him. On one occasion we were in an automatic car wash and midway through the cycle, with the fast-moving metal machinery roaring away all around us he decided to open the door and get out. I screamed at him to stop, but he calmly followed his will. I drove forwards and leapt out of the car to get him; he was just wandering aimlessly along the road, no doubt wondering why he was wet.

He would also declare that he did not like things touching his skin and pull down or remove his trousers in the most inappropriate situations, and I frequently had to physically stop him from doing it. One wintry day I looked out of the window at the snowy scenes outside, and noticed people pointing at something near my house. I craned my neck and saw David wandering around wearing nothing but his boxer shorts. While I was dragging him back into the house, he asked me why all the people were pointing at him.

This instinct could also lead to clothing simply getting lost, as he would remove something and forget about it. I was forever having to replace lost items, another drain on our dwindling resources.

* * *

When I happened to mention Dr Bond's name in relation to the hospital, Dr Ingalls gave an involuntary smile; I asked if she knew him and she nodded, saying, "Let's just say Dr Bond and I have had a few differences of opinion in the past." She looked at me as if in thought and said, almost to herself, "So that's where he has gone." I was a little confused and pressed her further, but all I got out of her was that Dr Bond had once worked at this hospital. Something had obviously gone on, and I begged Dr Ingalls not to let whatever rancour hovered between them interfere with her decision to let David go to the unit. I pointed out that until now Dr Bond had been the only person to offer any constructive help and had, indeed, sent me her way.

She seemed convinced of David's obvious need, but we both knew that the ultimate decision rested with the bureaucrats at the health authority, despite the influence Mr Malcolm might have had. After a pause for thought, she sighed resignedly, before telling me that, as she saw it, David's chances of getting help in the short term were slim, as there was quite a waiting list of people whose needs were similar to − and sometimes more urgent than − David's, and funding was negligible for this kind of treatment. I nodded along, but felt confident that Mr Malcolm would not let us down.

* * *

The next morning I rang Mr Malcolm to thank him for what I saw as a promising development, and took the opportunity to ask him if he could press on with the acquisition of David's funding as his needs were becoming desperate. He seemed surprised to hear me asking about this, and told me that he had never made any financial promises, only an assurance that an assessment would be carried out. Finding the money for a lengthy rehabilitation programme, he said, was a completely different matter. I was dumbfounded. This did not sound like the assurance he had made earlier; I would not have allowed myself to get excited about yet another assessment. I must admit to flying into something of a tirade at him – he needed to know that he had told me two different stories and that this was not acceptable.

"What?" he returned, "you mean you want me to help you jump the queue? Surely I wouldn't have agreed to that." By now I was seething inside. Surely it was up to the health authority to make sure there were no queues. If they were short, they needed to apply for further funding. But no, as usual, it seemed that the needs of the brain damaged would always come after those of more visibly impaired people. I pointed out that David had long been in urgent need and that he would have been put 'in the queue' a long time ago were it not for a list of failures by the powers that be. His need was critical.

He told me he could help me no further and put the phone down.

The next time I went to see Dr Ingalls, she took one look at me and said, "You look disappointed. I can see it written all over your face. You've been in touch with Mr Malcolm, haven't you?"

"Yes," I replied, "and you were right. They aren't going to fund David's care."

"Ah," she interrupted, her finger almost wagging at me, "I don't think it's impossible – but it will be extremely difficult, and it will take time and effort." She went on to advise me that my next course of action should be to write to MPs, and that even though it was a slow process, it could pay dividends in the long term.

My next concern was that of receiving some kind of income – both David and I were feeling the pinch. He had been put on statutory sick pay at his place of work, but this would last a maximum of one year, and that time was nearly up. On several occasions I had tried to get some kind of benefits, only to be told that none would be forthcoming as long as David was receiving sick pay. His sick pay was just £52 per week, which did not cover his mortgage, let alone living expenses. Plus there was the small matter of David's not having any official recognition of actually being in medical need. Luckily David's employer was quite large and had its own personnel and physician, who agreed that he was in no fit state to work. The personnel department's attempts to contact Mr Winner had been greeted with angry rejection, and to their credit they did not take him at his word, as would have been beneficial to them. So there was no chance of having his sick pay topped up to living standards by the benefits agency, and when his eligibility for sick pay expired there was little chance of any kind of income being made available. He might even have been forced back into work, with potentially disastrous consequences.

I used the second meeting to ask Dr Ingalls, who had of course expressed support and saw David as someone in desperate need, for a letter stating that David was not fit to work. She agreed, and noted it down in her to-do list.

We got talking about the centre, and Dr Ingalls expressed frustration at the lack of funding available considering the number of people in dire need. She explained that there was a limited pot of money every year, and that an application had to be made annually to receive funding over and above what was already given. For several years she had tried and failed to get a specialist unit within her area, as Badgers' Edge, her outpatients' clinic, was too far for locals to visit. What made it harder to bear was that these were times of amazing advances in the treatment of serious brain damage. All over the world, fabulous new developments and promising experimental results were ever pushing outwards the boundaries of possibility. And all the time, funding was being squeezed to collapsing point, resulting in waiting lists and missed opportunities in such a time-critical area of medicine. And even with emergency surgery and short-term treatment taking such giant leaps for the few, the rehabilitation that was so essential to make the fullest possible recovery was even harder to secure. It was a sorry state.

I asked Dr Ingalls if she could herself open and run a rehabilitation centre; she nodded and said that in the end it would all come down to funding and the annual ritual of making the applications to central government departments. She then added, conspiratorially, that people who pushed too hard or kicked up too much of a fuss with a view to changing the status quo could often find themselves at the receiving end of a direct or implied threat to their future employment. The health service was run ultimately by government policies and budgets, and the people actually performing the healthcare had little say in the direction of their area of expertise.

"But there's nothing to stop *me* from writing to my MP, is there?" I asked, recalling the advice she had given me at our last meeting. "What do I have to lose? As it happens, I really am planning to take my case to the highest authorities now."

She nodded again. I do not think she was even prepared to speak about it, and understandably so.

When Dr Bond came up in conversation, she asked me if I had any details on him. I said no, except for his card, which I handed to her. When she read it, a wry smile appeared on her face. "Oh, so he's calling himself a consultant these days, is he?"

"What do you mean?" I demanded.

"Well, really, you have to have been working for the NHS for two years before you can call yourself a consultant. Dr Bond certainly has not."

"Well he seems to know what he's talking about," I said. "He's one of the few people who have recognised that there is anything wrong with my son."

"Oh, I don't doubt for a second that he is competent. In fact I'm sure of it. He is probably more qualified for the job than many a bona fide consultant. But technically, this is misrepresentation, and if this gets out he could be in serious trouble."

It seemed to me that Dr Bond was making no secret of the fact that he was calling himself a consultant, to the degree of having cards printed, but this revelation still shocked me, because it seems nobody had actually bothered to check his credentials. When I started to contemplate things, it all fell into place. No wonder he had been so reluctant to have his name associated with David's case. He would surely be rumbled once news of his involvement scaled a few echelons. Despite this, I did not feel betrayed by Dr Bond; indeed, I saw this as little more than a technicality, a necessary bending of the rules in an organisation being brought to its knees by official procedure. And as Dr Ingalls herself admitted, his expertise on the subject was no doubt far in advance of any of those from the benefits agency or even David's GP. I regretted giving her the card, and hoped she would not be taking this further.

After the meeting was over I started putting into action her advice to write to MPs, and not just the ones with an interest geographically or by association with healthcare. I would need as many as possible on my side, as the House of Commons is a place where numbers count and opportunities to put a specific point across are rare. I would receive positive responses from Sir Charles Western, Peter James, Paul McDonald and Sir Angus McPherson; my own constituency's MP, Gordon Fielding, was at that time at a critical phase in his fight with cancer and was very ill, so I decided not to trouble him.

It seems that the advice was sound, because as soon as the health authority received their letters from the MPs demanding action, things started moving. Suddenly they were compelled to tell me what had been happening all along regarding my case – that David's treatment funding was never in doubt, that my claim was already being processed and that I must have misunderstood what was going on because of my distressed state! I should not have been surprised at such a brazen U-turn, bordering on the downright dishonest, but I was. I spoke to Mr Malcolm on the phone and he told me to watch who I spoke to and what I said in future, as he had been told off because of all this. Sorry, Mr Malcolm, I thought, but my son's health will always take precedence over your career.

I had also written letters to officials in Whitehall, pointing out that mental healthcare was being seriously underfunded and that it needed urgent attention. I received a pretty standard reply, asking me not to worry myself with this matter because it was all being taken care of. The letter also urged me to concentrate on my own son, but by reading between the lines it became clear that what they were implying was that I should shut up, not rock the boat, and await funding for my own case. The threatening undertones were unmistakable.

Soon after my meeting, Dr Ingalls's letter arrived in the post. With this, one more small hope arrived, but the work I would have to do looked daunting.

I took Dr Ingalls's letter to the benefits agency, and in another minor triumph secured some short-term financial help. Depressingly, it turned out that David had been entitled all along but that errors had been made which had prevented him from receiving them. An apology was too much to expect, particularly after all the tribunals and examinations and phone calls and letters ... I never did receive any expression of regret.

Another contact I made with Social Services came in the shape of a Mr Ali when he called to ask if we could talk in person. I said yes, and he offered to come to my house. When he arrived he looked anxious, and it soon became clear why. He had been sent on a mission by the Director of Social Services to ask me to stop writing letters to Whitehall and MPs, as it was beginning to cause them no end of trouble, with important people asking questions and looking into their practices. I could barely stop myself from laughing at the bare-faced cheek of it all, but I left him in no doubt that I would stop writing awkward letters the moment my son was receiving the rehabilitation he needed. Just as had been the case with the health authority, he told me that the wheels were already in motion with David's case, and that I did not need to put pressure on anyone. He joked that I must have friends in high places. When I asked why, he said that payment for this kind of treatment was normally split half and half between Social Services and the health authority, but that this was a little-known fact. After all, they could not have *everyone* who was entitled claiming, could they?

I would later hear that the Director of Social Services who had sent Mr Ali had been suspended on full pay while under investigation for misappropriation of funds. About a year later he would return to his post for a short while before taking early retirement.

My next meeting with Dr Ingalls was more upbeat than the last; she congratulated me on my progress and I thanked her for her advice, which had really paid dividends. Our most pressing task was to choose the establishment at which David would receive his rehabilitation. She told me of a place called the Western Transitional Rehabilitation Centre (WTRC) which was in Waddington, some distance from where I lived. In her opinion, it was the best place. Having visited The Meadows Unit, I made it clear that that was my personal choice. She told me that several places had been under consideration, including one in Denton under one Tony Lyons, which was relatively new but had seen considerable success. She told me that the WTRC was new and therefore had no proven track record, but that the work that was pioneering, hugely promising and had had some favourable reports. The distance from home was troubling, but I nevertheless took the word of someone who I had grown to trust.

Mr Ali, David and I travelled to Waddington in September and had a look around the centre, meeting its clinical director Mr Andrew Johnson. He and Mr Ali agreed on the urgency of David's need, and said that treatment would probably take eighteen months but that after the first twelve-month period there would be an assessment; in general, he told me, treatment was very hands-on and was constantly being changed to address the client's needs. The bad news was that places at the centre were extremely limited and before David could be admitted, another client would have to leave. However, a new building a short distance away, Stanley House, was nearing completion, and this would greatly increase capacity. I would have liked at least an estimate of a potential starting date, but understood why it could not be given; although I was assured it would be before Christmas. So we went away and awaited a place becoming available.

By mid-November, almost six weeks later, I had not heard anything and the waiting had become unbearable. I called the WTRC and was told that there were still no openings, and that it was looking more like January before one might emerge.

I went straight to Dr Ingalls and asked her if she could write off the WTRC idea and go with my preference, The Meadows Unit, but before I could finish my sentence I noticed that a smile was appearing on her lips. She told me that Dr Bond was finished, and that the NHS had bought the outsources of The Meadows Unit. I was shocked, and she gleefully related the story of Dr Bond being exposed (by whom, I wonder?) and threatened with being sued unless he resigned immediately. I asked where Dr Bond was now. By now almost laughing, she told me that he was back where he belonged – working as an anaesthetist at a hospital.

Unable to wait a second longer, she said, "And guess who will be running the centre?" It was a rhetorical question; she knew I was aware of her ambitions. I nodded.

* * *

My life continued to be an unbearable drudge, looking after David around the clock, missing out on sleep and living with only a glimmering opportunity of hope in the distance that seemed to move further away whenever we approached. I felt like David would one day just flip, and not be able to go back, and that the longer he was denied his rehabilitation the more likely this outcome would be.

We got through a dreadful, depressing Christmas, and as soon as the New Year had begun I phoned Mr Johnson to ask if he could give me an estimate of when David would be admitted. This time he guessed at early summer. My whole body collapsed with despair. I was being fobbed off again, with nobody knowing or caring how my life had been destroyed.

I started letter writing again: MPs, health authorities and Social Services would all be made aware of my plight. I phoned Mr Malcolm to let him know, and he stopped me, saying that if I was making a complaint he would need it in writing. This I did, and received no response. I called his office only to find out that he had been replaced! Further correspondence would be to Kate McLaren. The result was the same, however: I would still have to wait until a place at WTRC became available. The earliest date they could give me was now May, but even this was far from assured. I didn't know why sending David to another centre was so out of the question, but I guessed it was probably down to money – either the fact that they had already paid £200 for the assessment or (more likely) because the longer David had to wait, the longer they could hold on to the funds.

As a result of my letters asking for the process to be accelerated or at least for me to be put in the picture, I received a letter from the health authority. One key passage read:

> *As you know, the delay is due to a combination of factors which include delays in existing clients completing their rehabilitation programmes and the need to temporarily reduce the numbers, whilst they open their new and additional facilities. I must ask*

you to continue to be patient as this unit is the one that all the professional staff feel is most appropriate for David.

The month of May came and went without any progress being made. In June I finally got a tentative date somewhere near the beginning of July, and on 3 July, David was finally admitted into the Western Transitional Rehabilitation Centre. Apparently funding had been arranged for the end of the previous year, but this had been withheld as the centre was still training its staff to the highly professional standard it required.

On that day, I was prepared to look only forward, to make a completely fresh start and forget about all that had gone on in the past.

It would not be long, however, before I would be retrospectively picking up on telltale signs and analysing every letter, phone call and meeting as the next stage of David's nightmare started to slip into view.

6

Rehabilitation?

Making giant steps, a little at a time

This was the strapline of the Western Transitional Rehabilitation Centre emblazoned on the front of its brochure. Every page painted an extra layer of reassurance, hope and professionalism, as the techniques in use there were spelled out comprehensively and in plain English. They seemed to fully understand that it is not only the clients who are undergoing rehabilitation; it is often those close to them too. In essence, however, the centre's mission was to take in brain-damaged people and, through patience, attention and medical assistance, let them return to being complete members of the community.

Every entry on the list of specific benefits seemed perfectly appropriate: reintegration into community activities; independence; improved behavioural self-control; improved cognitive skills; improved family living skills; de-institutionalisation; return to successful employment; improved social skills; specialised job retraining; better emotional adjustment; improved communication skills; goal-directed social and recreational activity. It was as if they had studied David and defined their policies to address his every need.

Their philosophy was to create a world inside their fences that was as normal as possible so that becoming used to that environment would be preparation enough to return to society – which would itself be gradually realised. It all seemed so logical; so simple. They could even provide job training after assessing the client's desires, abilities and skills.

With such intense, specialised and continuous efforts, what could possibly go wrong?

Where should I start?

* * *

On the day in July when David finally went into the WTRC, I had my first full night's sleep in years, such was the impact of the sense of calm that the centre had implanted into my being. My life ahead felt like a brand new diary on New Year's Day, empty yet full of opportunity, surprises and special occasions to be enjoyed. My sons still meant everything to me, of course, but now any time to do things I wanted to do, including getting back to work, was immensely desirable. The horrors of the past, even the recent past, became less intense and seemed to be shrinking almost overnight. David was not only receiving the care he so badly required, I told myself, he was receiving it in a clean and safe environment with skilled and trained staff, twenty-four hours a day.

It's hard to express fully how happy I was that day, and how I believed my life and those of my two sons were at last on the up. Yet because of the events of the past, with false starts, heartbreak and apathy being the result of every potentially positive development, I tried not to be foolishly optimistic – not just yet, anyway. In fact, I can go a little further: I had a niggling feeling at the back of my mind. A feeling that something was not right. Whenever it popped up, I smacked it back down again, convincing myself that my sensitivity was acute where David's health was concerned, and that after so much failure it could even be wise to have a little apprehension about every opportunity. Time would prove that my niggles were not baseless. They might have been triggered at my subconscious level, but they were real and trying to tell me something. Years earlier I might have acted on them, but for some reason I was willing to give the WTRC a chance.

David was allocated a 'case organiser', Mr John Watts a 'chief coach', Mr Karl Smith and a 'personal coach', Mr Sean Brown. As David had no short-term memory, he was made to literally carry it around with him in the form of notes and a schedule of events for each day. This, the team explained, would start him thinking for himself and getting into a routine. In theory, this would slowly lead to his not requiring notes at all, as his brain would start to develop its own 'pen and paper'.

He would also need to be trained to do the routine things that the rest of us take for granted, but which he had been rendered unable to do by the accident. The inevitable drawback of this process is that it is slow, painstaking and often frustrating, not only for the client but for the carer, too. The carer must have a nature given to patience, perseverance and respect for the client for it to work. Although good progress is almost guaranteed in most cases, there is no telling how long it can take – indeed, weeks, months and even years are sometimes required before the process can be deemed a success. That success is measured in terms of how much the client can be weaned off the assistance and how self-sufficient they are becoming.

Once functioning memory is restored (goes the theory), the more advanced aspects of rehabilitation can follow, for example the training for specific jobs or a return to education. Routine is key to the practice, and wavering too far from the routine can cause problems, hence the sheltered, protected and predictable environment.

Towards the end of the treatment, some employment or training might be found for the client in the locality of the centre, whereby assistance would never be far away but a vital step back into society would have been made. This arrangement also offered the client dignity and character-building, along with the practicalities.

And as for me, close to physical and mental exhaustion after the intense effort to single-handedly rehabilitate my son, the centre offered me the chance of a little relaxation and peace of mind, not to mention the opportunity to have a social occasion every now and again and to catch up with friends.

After looking into the possibility for some time, I also decided to start earning some money by doing some care work myself, as a care assistant in a local nursing home. I knew that there would be times when the experience could prove vital in the care of David. I started at the bottom but as time went on I was to find more regular work and pick up skills. I was also interested in seeing what kind of treatment I could expect for David. I would find out that the care industry is not called an industry for nothing. Cost-cutting is key, and generally comes before care provision, when in reality the care should be the basis for coming up with a budget and that budget should be sought. Every so often there would be a meeting where the managers would deliver some spiel on targets and such like, and then at the end they would ask if the staff had any concerns. Nobody seemed to raise any, so we would all leave. Once I dared to mention that I thought we were slightly understaffed and the query was noted without response, and of course nothing was ever done about it. That would have meant paying more money rather than trying to find ways of saving it.

The cost of David's treatment was one worry that I carried, however. At £1,300 per week, it was not cheap, and should funding be cut off at any time, as I am sure was possible, the treatment would come to an abrupt end as there was no way I could cover the costs. It also concerned me that the funding for David's treatment would probably have meant that someone else, or several people, might have had their own essential treatment delayed, but this was out of my control and I made a vow to myself that when this was all over I would devote some time to raising awareness of, and possibly money for, the cause.

* * *

Mr Brown, David's personal coach, was in the position of direct responsibility to David. Part of his job was to be with him at all times or at least to know precisely where David was and what he was doing at every moment of every day; since he needed to sleep and as he did not work every waking hour, this responsibility could be deputed to someone else. David and Mr Brown seemed to hit it off instantly, and before long David regarded him as more of a friend than his coach. This was, of course, all part of the treatment – the introduction of routine and personal comfort into his life – but I did think that the feeling was reciprocated. I was asked not to visit for the first four weeks as that would give David time to settle in and ensure that the new circumstances did not feel temporary. After that I could visit whenever I pleased.

Those four weeks passed, and although they seemed like much longer to me, I managed to pull through and as the day when I could see him drew closer I started to get excited.

My first vision of David after this month of longing made it all worth the wait. He seemed to have calmed down considerably, was pleased to see me and appeared to have made fantastic progress in such a short time. If this level of improvement can be maintained throughout the entirety of his treatment, I thought, things really are looking up.

I took him out for lunch and we chatted like any other mother and son; it was a lovely, memorable day that reinforced my conviction that the WTRC was doing a sterling job. Over the coming weeks my visits continued and each time I detected a slight improvement in all the aspects that had been adversely affecting him.

At the start of October, however, my faith in the centre was severely tested.

I found out that on the night of 30 September David had not slept at the centre but had stayed overnight at Mr Brown's home. This was not a policy of the WTRC, and they knew nothing about it. In fact, the way I found out was that David actually called to tell me to lie to anyone from the WTRC who asked about his whereabouts that weekend; he asked me to say that he had been staying at my house, as coaches were not allowed to take clients home and that Mr Brown would get in trouble if this got out. In fact, it was a sackable offence. I refused to play along with this ridiculous scheme, saying that if they were the rules then it was in nobody's long-term interest to break them.

Suspicion must have been in the air at the centre, because later that day someone from there phoned me and asked me directly if David had slept at my house that night. I was in no mood to save Mr Brown's skin, and told them the truth.

"What is going on?" I demanded.

"Oh, it's okay," said the voice on the line. "It's not your problem; it's an internal matter that needs clearing up."

This was not good enough. I made an appointment to see Mr Watts, the case organiser, to get to the bottom of this. We met and he related, in quite a matter-of-fact way, the following story.

One of the female coaches from the centre, Ms Jones, also happened to be Mr Brown's girlfriend, and they lived together in a house not far from the WTRC. They had been going through a rough patch in their relationship, and on the evening of the 30th, Mr Brown had taken David to his house and 'popped out' for some shopping, leaving David in alone. Soon after he left, Ms Jones came home, started drinking alcohol and gave some to David. When Mr Brown got back, a huge row had broken out, and Ms Jones stormed out of the house. Mr Brown then cooked a meal for himself and David, and just as they were finishing Ms Jones came back and Mr Brown went to bed. Ms Jones then took David into her bedroom. Mr Brown barged in to her room and yet another row broke out.

The following morning, Ms Jones reported Mr Brown for taking David home. Some personnel from the centre went to their home and took David back to the centre.

Ms Jones was instantly dismissed for professional misconduct, and Mr Brown was suspended while enquiries were made. At the very least it should have been the other way round, but I would have preferred to see them both dismissed for taking David home, plying him with alcohol and potentially taking him to bed.

This reminded me of one occasion when I had met Ms Jones at the centre. I had met her several times before and although she seemed pleasant enough, she always struck me as being a little evasive. But on this particular occasion she shocked me by showing me the knife she carried with her. When I asked why, she said that it was for her own protection. I mentioned this to other staff members and they laughed it off.

Mr Watts told me that Ms Jones had in fact had psychological problems herself and was on medication, as was Mr Brown, who had had a nervous breakdown. When he asked me not to mention this to anyone, to keep it between me and him, alarm bells sounded in my mind.

More worryingly, I discovered that rumours abounded that Mr Brown's attachment to David was more than professional or even amicable – he had developed a strong sexual attraction towards him, and had become somewhat possessive of David, resenting anyone else dealing with him. I can only guess at what his ulterior motives had been when he took David home with him, and wondered if Ms Jones had taken him into her room for his own protection.

Soon after this occurrence, I made my misgivings about the establishment clear to Mr Johnson, the clinical director, letting it be known that I did not feel that my son was being kept in a safe environment. He tried to reassure me by telling me that he agreed with me that what had happened was completely unacceptable, and that Mr Brown had been dismissed for gross professional misconduct. He tried to play down events, describing them as a hiccup, a one-off, and assuring me that vigilance would from then on play a greater part in David's care.

This was a small comfort, but a comfort nonetheless. That is until my phone rang a few days later.

The voice on the other end was familiar but it was not until its owner declared himself as being Mr Brown that my heart leapt.

"Listen," he said. "I'm taking the WTRC to a tribunal for unfair dismissal. You have no idea what is going on in that centre. I don't want to alarm you, but I believe that David's life is in danger and the longer he is there the greater the chances he will be hurt."

"What should I do?" I asked, wondering what all this was leading to.

"I will look after David at my house," he suggested. "You can pay me and I'll take better care of him than the centre ever could. I won't charge anywhere near what they do. I can do other work as well."

Stunning though this proposal was, I was careful not to dismiss it out of hand. As well as being sympathetic to someone who had previously suffered from mental problems, I saw Mr Brown as an insider who knew what was going on in the centre. I had been lied to and fobbed off enough times by medical professionals to pay little heed to their stories. And who was to say that the rumours of Mr Brown's attraction to David had not been initiated by the centre itself?

My patience and open-mindedness soon ran out when Mr Brown started phoning me at all hours, sometimes at dead of night, telling me that David was in mortal danger. This was disturbing as well as being extremely annoying.

I phoned the clinical director, Mr Andrew Johnson, voiced my concerns and arranged a meeting. When I asked why I was constantly being told that David's life was in danger, Mr Johnson told me that Mr Brown was a sick man, and that I was not to pay any heed to what he said.

Every logical impulse I had told me to grab David and drag him out of the centre as quickly as I could, but I recalled Dr Ingalls's warning that the centre was David's only hope of receiving funding from the NHS or Social Services. Once again I was left with no choice but to keep going as things were, but I made sure I would be keeping a very close eye on things and looking out for any further evidence that things were not right.

* * *

The Sea World Centre in Brampton is a tourist attraction where exotic and wonderful creatures of the deep can be viewed, and when David was told that this could be the location for his first work placement, he was overjoyed. If he passed the interview he could work there two days a week, and his excitement at the prospect was unmistakable. But just before the day of the interview it was cancelled by the centre pending the result of a problem with the Brown and Jones situation. David had set his heart on the placement. It was not the sort of place he had even hoped for at the start of his treatment, and he saw it as a truly unique opportunity. It was worrying to see how he reacted to the news; the tranquillity, predictability and routine that had been a constant backdrop were in danger of being neutralised. Fortunately, after the initial disappointment, he did appear to rally. But this kind of thing must not happen again.

* * *

With this drama over and all the villains seemingly off the stage, David was taken under the wing of Karl Smith, the chief coach, and once again he started to show remarkable progress. In fact, it made me realise that the progress I had observed during his time with Mr Brown had not in fact been all that satisfactory. What is more, Karl was refreshingly open to contact and I could ask him whatever question I liked with regard to David and he would give me a straight and honest answer. Of course, he could not look after David twenty-four hours a day, but whenever he was occupied, he would be keeping his eye on proceedings and would delegate the tasks only to those he knew were capable. This was a critical phase in David's rehabilitation – he was being instructed in personal hygiene, which was still not up to acceptable standards, and he had to keep working on essential daily tasks to get some routine back into his life.

Every morning there was a meeting to decide on the tasks for that day, starting with breakfast. Clients had to write down the timetable, which was particularly difficult for David as his writing ability had been all but lost; they could then use it as a reference source when they lost their way, which was almost inevitable. In addition, the timetable made sure that David kept an eye on what time of day it was, yet another skill most of us take for granted but which the accident had sadly taken away from him. He loved to feed the chickens and do gardening, both of which, interestingly, are activities whose long-term benefits are much more pronounced than the short-term ones. However, there was no doubt that his short-term memory was improving, and that was a major step. It made having a conversation slightly easier as the number and size of things he could retain slowly grew.

I would visit David most weekends, and towards the end of his time at the centre he would sometimes come home for the weekend as long as I could pick him up.

By November, his memory and awareness had improved dramatically. This was a double-edged sword as his own improvement made him more receptive to the conditions of the people he had made friends with, and as many of them were in a bad way, it could make him feel frustrated and upset.

His left-side weakness remained, and would occasionally give rise to quite a pronounced limping, but on the whole, the casual observer would not have noticed anything wrong with him. This was ironic, as it meant people would often not believe that he was seriously ill. Dr Ingalls used the term 'walking wounded' to describe people in this state, and I gradually began to understand what she meant. Apart from the weakness, or more accurately its visible manifestations, David looked like a healthy young man, and in some ways I believe that it was the hidden nature of his condition that had made a succession of potential funders and medics step back from offering assistance. I recalled reading about the 10,000 people in the UK who suffer moderate brain damage every year, and the 4,500 whose damage was more serious, and pitied them if they were receiving the same help as David had before he came to the WTRC. Unfortunately, most never get the lucky break, and end up homeless, in prison or in psychiatric units. And that is not to mention the danger many of them pose to the general public; I had seen my own loving, calm son display shocking violence and a short temper, so how someone with a less serene demeanour could turn is the stuff of nightmares. Another irony is that, as science advances, more and more victims of head injury could make great progress if only the will and the understanding was there – but these invisible wounds will always receive less pity than the more obvious ones, when in fact they should be on an equal footing.

How can this lack of care and funding in our supposedly civilised society be tolerated?

* * *

With David's awareness of the agony of his friends growing daily, and the resulting depression appearing to be hindering his own progress, the decision was made to move him to another part of the centre several miles away, Stanley House.

This was quite a big step in his rehabilitation, because for the first time he would live in his own self-contained apartment. When he showed me round, I was shocked, however, to see that in the kitchen was a very frightening-looking knife set, the handles of the instruments extending out of the block.

"They are not here all the time, are they?" I asked.

"Oh, yes," he cheerfully replied. "And watch!"

He proceeded to slice easily through a dishcloth as though it were made of paper, and perhaps got a mischievous thrill out of the look that must have appeared on my face. I had seen his attempts to cook when he had been in my house and it was terrifying to watch him, with his weakness and clumsiness, making delicate judgements with boiling water, oven doors and rapier-sharp blades.

I brought it up with the person in charge at Stanley House, and as usual it was laughed off. There was, I was assured, somebody with David at all times, so there was little chance of him attempting to use the knives for cooking. It put my mind at rest a little.

Apart from the knives, the place seemed like a clean, modern and spacious place to live, with quite large gardens. It was set near to a moderately sized patch of woodland, which would later be the source of another stressful time for David, but at first gave the centre a peaceful feel. It seemed that the woodland had been protected and various planning applications rejected. However, the national shortage of residential rehabilitation units (and possibly the fact that the millionaire owner, Tony Aitken, was married to a high-ranking member of the local constabulary) meant that later not only was planning permission granted but that the land was bought at a steal and more units built on the woodland. In addition, the siting of Stanley House caused problems with the locals, partly because it cut off their route to the woods where they would walk.

I did regret that Karl would not be looking after David, as the progress they had made together had been promising. When I said so, his reply painted a picture of understaffing, stress and burn-out, caused partly by the paltry wages received by professional carers and the resulting need to work many hours' overtime. Most would not last more than a year or two, and moved on to more lucrative professions.

This did seem to answer one of the things that had been playing on my mind over the previous months: the distinct lack of staff available when required. No doubt the staffing of the centre was more like a conveyer belt, with new staff joining to fill the gaps left by those leaving. It also made me question whether the WTRC's assertion that they only employ fully qualified staff was – or could possibly have been – true. A conversation I had had with Mr Brown a while back had not really hit home, but I did remember him saying that he had been a gardener before starting at the centre, and that he was, to all intents and purposes, learning the job as he went along. I had assumed that he would still have been under close supervision from his superiors, but knowing about the employment situation, I now doubted that this had been the case. And the way he acted support this.

As I drove home that night I started to feel like I had actually been betrayed by the WTRC, and that the claims made in their glossy brochure were fraudulent. When I considered how much is charged for the privilege of having your loved ones cared for by these 'highly trained, professional carers', to hear that the carers themselves are practically taken from the Job Centre, given no training and then forced to live on a pittance, made me feel sick.

The postponed interview with the Sea World Centre finally went ahead and David got through and took the job, working two days a week. He absolutely adored it there, to the point where he developed ambitions to stay there after his placement if it was possible. Working with the animals was something of a dream David never knew he had, and perhaps if his career had taken another turn, he might have ended up in that field. To hear him gushing about his day, about feeding sharks and the other fish, it was impossible not to become overjoyed for him, especially after his past few years. It is strange how the thought of your son slicing bread can fill you with dread but the idea of throwing food into a pool of live sharks can bring a warm smile to your face.

But David's life being what it was, the joy was to be short-lived. One morning at 9.45 I was called by the operator and asked if I could accept a reverse-charge call from Brampton. It was David, and he wanted me to ring the WTRC to get someone to pick him up.

"But you're in work today!" I exclaimed, wondering if his memory had taken a sudden lapse back to how it had been.

With his voice breaking up, and clearly fighting back tears, David explained that he had been dismissed. Apparently he had not turned up on three consecutive Saturdays, and on many occasions he had arrived late. What was galling was the fact that on every occasion he had been up and ready to go, but there had been nobody at Stanley House to drive him to Brampton to work. The fish not being fed in the morning would put the whole day out of sync, and it was therefore vital that he was there on time. He said that the manager of the Sea World Centre, Rob Davis, had screamed at him to leave the premises, a humiliating and stressful experience. I found myself fighting back tears; I knew how much he loved the work.

I composed myself but was worried that he might do something stupid, so told him to go and get a coffee while I phoned the WTRC; but he replied he had no money to his name, hence the reverse-charge call. I instructed him to stay where he was, and called the WTRC.

The clinical director, Mr Johnson, seemed quite shocked to hear about what had happened. I told him I was appalled that David has basically been dropped off in Brampton with no money and no means of transport and he seemed to agree that the situation was not acceptable. He said he would ring back shortly and hung up. When he called back he said he was very upset, as he had personally arranged the placement with Rob Davis, and part of the arrangement was that if ever David fell below standard or if there was any disciplinary action to be taken, Mr Davis was not to confront David personally with it, but to go through him. Mr Davis had expressed exasperation at David's attendance, particularly when he had not been informed that David could not make it to work. He had also told Mr Johnson that he would not be taking on any more placements from the WTRC and that their working relationship was over.

Once again the WTRC had let me down; the financial bonds that committed me to the centre were all that stopped me taking David back.

I called Rob Davis as soon as this call ended. I needed to get to the bottom of this, and express my disgust at the way he had treated David. His indifference made the staff at the hospitals and benefits agencies seem positively angelic. He told me that he did not care if David was brain damaged, he only worked two days a week and would not be missed, and that if I wanted to complain I should go ahead, because it would not bother him in the least. When I asked if he knew the potential consequences of his actions – throwing a penniless, brain-damaged, distressed and vulnerable young man onto the street to make his way home – he slammed the phone down on me. For the first time in quite a while, I broke down and sobbed uncontrollably.

* * *

This incident took David backwards in his rehabilitation. When I saw him at weekends he seemed apathetic and no longer wanted to be at the centre. His confidence had taken a knock, and the dreadful way he had been treated no doubt accounted for part of this. On my visits I also began to feel a certain unease; it was due to little actions such as staff members avoiding eye contact, but it was hard to avoid feeling this sense of foreboding whenever I went there. Friction between staff members was always in the air, too.

My next shock came when David told me that on numerous occasions *he* had been asked to look after other clients. In other words, there was a hierarchy of illness, and as you recovered you were expected to care for those deemed worse than you. As well as being thoroughly unacceptable from a care standpoint, it was highly annoying to think that the WTRC was being paid an awful lot of money to look after these needy people, and was actually asking clients to look after each other. When I raised the issue with Karl Smith he put it down to a misunderstanding, saying that the instruction had been given by a trainee coach and that it would not happen again.

On another occasion staff at the centre pestered David to do some painting and decorating on the building, as they knew he had done some of the trade in the past. When I told them that under no circumstances was he to perform such tasks, knowing the possible risks, they merely laughed. They obviously did not like me telling them what to do, and I must admit that my raising the issue embarrassed David somewhat; but it had to be done.

After nine months at the centre, it was decided that David's short-term memory was good enough to allow him to make his own way home at weekends (instead of me having to collect him from the centre) and this usually meant a train journey. The first time I met him at the station; the second time he got a taxi. It was a little worrying, but I had to bow to their greater knowledge of David's condition, despite all I had experienced.

Again, though, David found himself being put in a position of authority. On two occasions he was accompanied on his home visits by Jimmy Hunt, a fellow client from the WTRC, but one who had severe emotional problems. They arrived penniless and without supervision, and the fact that Jimmy would be with David was not announced to me. I had to provide them with the cash to get back to the centre. The first time he came, I rang the WTRC to complain, and they actually took it out on him, punishing him by confining him to the unit. This distressed him so much that he went to a motorway bridge and threatened to throw himself under the oncoming vehicles, resulting in the motorway being closed and hours of negotiations to talk him down from his precarious perch that he could easily have fallen from. Of course, when he turned up for the second time I did not dare complain.

Jimmy had severe facial disabilities after an accident with a train, and I pitied him immensely and did quite like him, although he had a very short fuse and could go into a rage at the slightest provocation, something I was not able to deal with. Clearly the WTRC should have been looking after him, especially in view of this aspect of his personality; what made it worse was that certain heartless members of the public would actually call him names and hurl abuse at him.

* * *

David had always had a love of wildlife, but did believe that animals in a natural habitat should be left to their own devices, and that nature's course would maintain balance. When watching wildlife shows on TV where stalking lions would hunt down and kill their prey, I would cover my face and wonder why the crew did not intervene. Pragmatic David would sit there and say that that is the way nature is and has been for millions of years and will continue when the cameras are switched off. He also disliked human interference because it could remove the healthy apprehension creatures have for humans. Domesticated animals were one thing, but making wild animals trust humans, when there are many who would do them harm, always grated on David.

So when certain members of the centre started saving scraps of their meals and leaving them outside to feed the family of foxes that lived in the woods, David stood up for his beliefs and told them to stop. They were having none of it, and told him to mind his own business. The clients would sometimes watch the foxes come out at night – and sometimes during the day – to see what had been left out for them. The adult foxes were always wary, but the cubs would head straight to the morsels without fear, and David knew that it would end in tears. His fears were proved right. One day several of the clients were sobbing and looking out of the window when David arrived in the room. He looked out and saw a dead fox cub in the middle of the lawn. Someone had been able to walk right up to it and shoot it in the head. He screamed at the others and blamed them for letting this happen.

As quite often happened with stressful events, it made him

78   *Return from Nowhere*

withdraw into himself and seemed to knock back any progress he had made by several months. When I took him for a meal he opened up a little and told me all about the foxes; then he told me another horrifying story.

The locals had started to trespass on the grounds and use it as a shortcut to the woods. Nobody liked to see people cutting through the grounds but the staff did nothing about it. On one occasion David confronted a trespasser and was threatened with a knife. On another he had a handgun pulled on him, and a few times he had shotguns pointed at him if he tried to stop people using the grounds of this supposedly secure site. When I said I would bring it up with Mr Johnson he begged me not to, and promised that he would run away if I did. I got the impression that he was more scared of the staff there than he was of the strangers who were threatening him.

I did have a quiet word with Karl, whom I trusted, and he told me that the centre had once used private security guards but as a cost-cutting measure they had got rid of them and asked the carers and clients to be vigilant. Yet again the WTRC was getting its clients to perform tasks that should have been done by professionals. I wondered where all the money was going. I also worried that the location of David's apartment made it difficult to keep an eye on, as it wasn't visible from the main building so I made sure I visited at least once a week to ensure everything was okay.

Two distressing things happened over the following weeks. First, another client started throwing stones at David's window. When he looked out he saw the man rolling about in the mud in the pouring rain, completely unsupervised and unmissed. Shortly after, there was a knock on his door, and when David asked who was there the reply came that it was Keith Duke; David realised it was he who had been rolling around outside. Keith believed he was a homosexual, uninhibited because of his head injury, and had quite openly asked David to engage in sexual acts with him; indeed, he had taken quite a shine to my son, although David was not interested and tried firmly to tell him so. Keith kept shouting that it was raining and begging David to let him in, but David adamantly resisted. Eventually, though, Keith gave up, but after he left, David felt quite nervous; this incident had unsettled him and he could not sleep. This was supposed to be a facility where supervision took place twenty-four hours a day, yet Keith had for some time been completely free to do whatever he wanted.

I brought the subject up with my regular progress meeting with Mr Johnson a few days later. He told me Keith wasn't really homosexual, but following a night out with his mates, he had been severely beaten at a takeaway and suffered brain damage, and it was since this incident that he believed he was. He assured me that nothing like this would happen again and that the one-to-one care would be fortified. He had, he said, apologised to David for the incident, and David had accepted his apology. In Johnson's world, all sorts of things could be allowed to happen as long as they were dealt with in a gentlemanly apology. The fact that the promised round-the-clock supervision was not being delivered was of little relevance to him. Things would all work out fine in the end, he assumed.

But in Keith Duke's case, Johnson's optimism would be found to be extremely shallow and dangerous. Months after this incident, Keith Duke was found murdered in Stanley House.

I only heard about the murder when it appeared on the television news. David was home for Christmas and he shouted to me while I was in the kitchen. I could not believe what I had just seen, but when it sank in, I felt sick, scared and angry, and cried for hours for that poor man. This vulnerable and troubled man, for whose care someone was paying nearly £70,000 per year, had been neglected by his so-called carers and effectively left to fend for himself among other disturbed people. The news took me back to one of those occasions that you write off as insignificant at the time but which became magnified and intensified with new revelations. I remember two carers walking along, deep in conversation. Keith had spoken to one of them and in reply got hit over the head with a rolled-up newspaper and told not to be stupid. The only other time I had seen Keith was when I had gone to pick David up from the centre. He was standing outside the door and he asked if he could come with us. He told David he was lucky to be going home. I clearly remember him wearing a striped tee-shirt and blue jeans and waving to us as we left. That was the last time I saw him.

Keith ended up in the WTRC when he and some friends had gone to the pub and had decided to get a takeaway on the way home. There they had got into an argument and ultimately a fight, which had resulted in the brain haemorrhage that put him in hospital. I do not know who started the fight or what kind of person Keith was before the incident, but ultimately something that had happened over a split second some time ago had ended up costing him his life in a most horrific way. On the night of the murder he had been made to strip naked by another client and then forced outside where he was stabbed to death and had his lifeless body stuffed into a drainage pipe that was lying in a construction area.

This event was shocking enough for anyone to learn, but for me, the knowledge that it could just as easily have been my son was hard to bear.

This and all the other episodes that I describe – plus those I have not, and probably many I do not know about – could lead to no conclusion other than that the management of the WTRC did not care for its clients or even for the contractual obligations that were signed on their admittance, as spelled out in the brochure. The whole project seemed to be a moneymaking scheme, as evidenced by the thoughtless cost-cutting measures that had ultimately led to a death and endless counts of putting the clients in danger. The security guard issue is a case in point. They were being paid a fairly low hourly rate to guard the premises and by all accounts were doing a good job, but the management deemed it better to let the staff and clients maintain security. Was this a sensible, thought-out move or a cynical way to save money? It's not a hard question to answer. Asking the clients to perform odd jobs – such as painting and even driving the minibus – and to look after one another was of no benefit to anyone but the owners.

We must not forget Mr Johnson's role in all of this, too. He was very adept at deflecting blame that was clearly his, and implanting reassuring words in the minds of anyone who went to him with a worry, but it would be difficult to pinpoint what he actually did at the centre. Considering he was supposed to be one of the top three clinical psychologists in the country, he had no qualms about delegating vital tasks to people ill-prepared to perform them. I have little doubt that his ideas and methods might well have been sound, and when progress was made with my son, it was striking. But I believe he got sucked into a celebrity lifestyle, giving talks and appearing on TV, and saw the day-to-day running of the centre as somewhat mundane. His self-aggrandisement soon turned to arrogance, and he eventually started to talk down to both clients and their concerned relatives.

Slowly, details of Mr Johnson's tacit responsibility for Keith's murder came out, and it became clear that the whole thing was depressingly avoidable. Mr Johnson was so assured of his unfailing abilities in the field of rehabilitation that he offered to take on a 'hopeless case' to prove to his adoring followers that he was a great innovator. The person in question was called Adrian, and he was in a secure remand centre for an attempted murder. Without doubt, he was a thug and a bully, and as soon as he entered the WTRC he took over. Everyone, including the staff, was terrified of him. He would steal money and property without even attempting to conceal it, and ran the place like his own domain. A lot of the clients were wheelchair-bound, and could do nothing to avoid him, but even the physically strong clients who were in friendly groups were powerless to defeat him. Mr Johnson, of course, did not have to worry, because he would have very little contact with Adrian. In fact, it seems that very few people had any contact with him, which was partly how he managed to rule the centre as he did.

Eventually Adrian started to single out Keith, and treated him even worse than he did everyone else, perhaps because of his sexuality. He would regularly threaten him with death, often in front of the staff members who, by all accounts, laughed at the threats. I will never know if it was a complaint about the bullying that earned Keith a smack across the head with a rolled-up newspaper, but this would certainly exemplify the way the staff dealt with problems brought to them by these vulnerable and often frightened people.

David had mentioned the fact that there was a potential murderer wandering among them, and that he was causing everyone problems, so I had taken the issue up with Mr Johnson. He had told me that he understood my concerns but that this was a special case and that he really would be supervised one-on-one, twenty-four hours a day. Of course, it turned out to be just another lie, and it was no doubt motivated by a desire to keep costs down.

Several of the families and I wrote to the centre and the health authorities to voice our concerns about the goings-on at the WTRC. I was told that there was to be a public meeting to address the issues and to reassure everyone, but when I phoned to get details I was told that the meeting was going to be held in private after all.

Apparently a 215-page report was produced covering issues raised by the case. I desperately wanted to read it, and called the local health authority to ask to see it. The man on the end of the line just said it was not possible and put the phone down on me.

This whole thing was beginning to look like a massive cover-up. And you would have to be incredibly naïve to think that it had nothing to do with the fact that the owner, Mr Aitken, was a hugely wealthy and influential man, whose wife was high up in the local police establishment.

The only time I was asked for my input was when I received a questionnaire, presumably sent to all family members, asking if I felt that there were any matters I would like to raise. I consulted my solicitor and was advised not to answer, as I was starting to put together evidence on my son's behalf.

I did find out snippets of the report, for example its finding that the staff at the WTRC did not seem to know what their job entailed, and there was a recommendation to fix this. So much for highly qualified staff.

In the immediate wake of the murder, while the news media were still interested in the story, the WTRC made it known that they blamed Karl Smith for the oversights, as he was supposed to be in charge of Adrian. He was sacrificed to save the centre's image; of that I have no doubt. Sadly, Karl was the one person I trusted the most there. He would not have been on good pay but always came across as being the most naturally caring and sympathetic member of staff, even though he might well have been part of the problem on this occasion. But of course anyone who might have thought twice about sending their family members to the £1,300-a-week centre might have had their minds put at rest by this seemingly decisive action, misguided though it would

Rehabilitation? **83**

have been. Several families did remove their relatives from the centre after the murder. They knew what was going on, of course, and this was the final shock.

I was to discover that on the night of the murder, the staff of the centre were drinking beer and playing cards, oblivious to the horrors taking place yards away. Over the years I would hear all sorts of stories about the apathy and cruelty the staff displayed towards the clients. I will never forget how they once told a client that if he sang like Elvis they would give him a Mars Bar. He really did not want to do it as he was quite shy and withdrawn, and it would have been humiliating. But they pestered him and dangled the Mars Bar in front of him until, probably to shut them up, he did his embarrassing rendition at which the whole place burst into uproarious laughter and the poor man slunk away to hide in a corner. This kind of behaviour does not happen spontaneously and simultaneously among a group of people, particularly carers, so the only conclusion that can be drawn is that such an attitude towards the clients was institutionalised, and that complaints would be treated with contempt.

My previously chatty and affable son had, after promising boosts in his confidence and abilities, almost returned to where he was when he entered the centre – withdrawn, truculent and difficult. I knew there was something on his mind, and finally persuaded him to tell me what it was, on condition that I told no one. He revealed to me that the staff members were regularly beating up a certain client (Jack) and that once he had walked in on them doing it. They had him on the floor and were surrounding him and laying into him. David told them to stop but they shouted at him to get out and not mention it to anyone, but he had gone to Mr Johnson, who told him that he knew nothing about why the man was being disciplined and that it was nothing to do with David. He told David not to mention it to anyone, and that if he did, Mr Johnson would deny it, and put it down to David's brain damage. (The sad thing was, Jack had been moved to the WTRC for his own safety, as he was being beaten at the previous unit.)

David genuinely believed that he was in danger, and begged me to take him out of the centre. But for all the dreadful things that had gone on, I was still convinced that the centre was the right place for David. Of course with hindsight, and reading about the succession of incidents crammed into this chapter, this seems ill-considered. But I had seen progress while he had been there, and the events had taken place over a relatively long time span. I remained convinced that this was David's only hope and that as long as I remained extra vigilant, it could still be a success. If only I had been blessed with hindsight back then, although I had been told that this was David's only option, and if he left there, funding would be stopped.

When I noticed that David was suffering small seizures, I became quite concerned, and it was only during one chance occasion that I discovered why. We were on one of our regular visits to the neurologist when David started experiencing a seizure; it was then that I found out that his prescription of Epilim had been stopped at the behest of the centre's penny-pinching owner, Mr Aitken. This clearly contravened the rule that any changes to medication would have to be approved by a consultant. The seriousness of this decision cannot be overstated – David could have died had a severe seizure occurred.

As soon as I got home from the meeting I made a call to Mr Aitken. It was hard to keep my emotions in check as I asked him if he knew that Epilim was to prevent fits, and if he knew how much of a risk he was taking.

"The GP had already said he could come off it. And if David was on Epilim he would not be able to drive the minibus!" he said.

"He shouldn't be driving any minibuses," I snapped. "In your literature it distinctly stated that a consultant would be provided if necessary."

"Well it wasn't necessary," he said, beginning to sound agitated.

"Are you a consultant? Are you qualified?" I asked, knowing the answer.

"Do you know who you are talking to?" he screamed back.

"Yes," I said, "only too well." As I put the receiver down I could still hear his voice yelling back at me.

Mr Aitken was planning to use David as an example of a success story thanks to his wonderful establishment. "Look what can be achieved with

Rehabilitation? 85

our structured programme" would have read the literature. No doubt they would have vastly overplayed the state David was in at the start and the amazing transformation just £70,000 – sorry, twelve months – later. Of course, David would have been the number one choice merely because of his lack of physical impairments. It is sickening to think that he would have been used this way, and that the less photogenic clients would have been seen, in commercial terms, as less than profitable.

* * *

Over the previous few months, the centre had been considering moving David to live independently in his own flat. This meant that a suitable place had to be found reasonably close to the centre, but it represented a major step, and I think that the prospect of moving out of the centre that had so many bad memories attached to it was a fillip to David, and it kept him going.

In September we got the news that a suitable house had been found and he moved in very soon afterwards. Several days after the move there was a violent robbery in the room he had occupied in the centre. David's lucky escape was another client's nightmare; although there was fortunately no serious injury or death, a sum of money and a wristwatch were taken. The client's parents promptly took him out of the centre as a residential client and he became a day client, which meant being dropped off and picked up every day. I had always been concerned that David's flat, situated at the end of a corridor, was somewhat isolated and out of view, and this was no doubt a factor in the assailant's choice of target.

As soon as David was in the house he became eligible for state benefits, and not surprisingly the centre wasted no time in getting this aspect of his welfare sorted out. His move was so quick that I had not even seen the new house by the time he had moved in. I called to ask how it was and he hesitantly replied that it was all right. But within a few days he had encountered a man on the roof trying to break in; the WTRC was called and passed the matter to the police. Shortly after, he returned to find two youths attempting to break in. He confronted them, expecting them to scarper, but instead they threatened him and told him they would be back. He was alone and terrified; this was effectively the first time he had lived alone since the day before his fateful holiday, and living alone after being looked after for so long can be disconcerting at the best of times. After he called me in such distress, I called the WTRC. It was six o'clock in the evening and they said nobody could help right then and asked me to call again in an hour. This I did; they said they would get back to me. Another hour passed and David called again, pleading for some help. I went straight there, and at the side of the house two youths were fighting and swearing. I just wanted to reach David, and it was only when I got close to them that I realised that one of them was brandishing a knife. One stepped into my way. I shouted at him to move and he did – I darted to David's door. I started banging but there was no response. My heart was pounding and I started banging harder and harder until I noticed a twitch of the curtain. He opened the door and as soon as I ran in he slammed it behind me.

He seemed strangely relieved that the pair were fighting each other and not attempting to gain entry to his house, and I calmed down enough to realise that there was a disgusting musty smell in the house. David said it had been there since he moved in, but I found it so powerful that I had to go back outside for a few minutes for some fresh air. David told me that he would have opened the windows but since he had almost been broken into twice to his knowledge, he had not dared. He told me he had also barely slept because every sound he heard triggered a fear response that took hours to come down from. He then took me upstairs and showed me the collapsed ceiling where the burglars had attempted to gain entry.

I told David to sit down while I got him a drink. Just as I reached the kitchen something fell from above; I jumped and screamed. It was some kind of insect, which scurried away. David told me it was harmless and that there were lots of them. I looked up and saw a scene that will never leave me – the ceiling was alive with a morass of black, crawling bugs. I saw cockroaches, spiders and all manner of unidentifiable creatures and I instantly wanted to throw up. Again I opened the door and stood in the doorway illogical thought this may seem.

"David, pack your bags. We're leaving," I announced.

"Are you joking?" he asked, obviously overjoyed at the prospect.

Rehabilitation? 87

But this was no joke. He ran upstairs and I stayed where I was, surveying the rotting skirting boards, peeling wallpaper, filthy carpets and signs of dampness everywhere. I also noticed that it was freezing cold, which would not have helped matters.

He called me upstairs and reluctantly I left the safety of a knife fight to brave the bedroom. It was crammed full of boxes, bags and suitcases.

"Whose are these?" I asked.

"Oh, they're the previous occupant's," he replied. "I'm waiting for the WTRC to come and pick it all up."

"But what does it have to do with them?" I asked.

"Well the previous occupant was from there," he said.

I let out a sigh. The WTRC had told me that we were lucky to have landed such a house, as the area was highly sought after and there were not many places to rent. This was clearly a lie. The house was located in one of the most notorious estates in the area, and the pub opposite was the scene of brawls and rows every single night. The previous tenant, a woman living on her own, had fled after constant harassment, break-in attempts and being the target of games of 'knock and run' by the local youths.

I had started loading up the car with David's things when a police car screeched to a halt in a cloud of burning rubber.

"Are there two people fighting with knives?" he asked me.

"There were, yes, but they ran off that way," I answered. He seemed concerned, and not without reason. Who knows where they had gone or what were their intentions? "Look, I'm sorry, but I just want to get my son out of this dreadful place," I said, beginning to turn away.

"Tell, me about it," he said, shaking his head in despair. "We get called to this estate all the time, and we have to go to a call at that pub over there every night. We want it closed down."

It is not hard to imagine how distressing this all was, and it made a mockery of the WTRC's pledge to find a peaceful and predictable place for recovery and rehabilitation.

On the way home David asked me if we could stop for a meal. I asked if he was hungry and he said he only got £5 a day for gardening, and that was meant to cover all his food and bus fares. That day he had lost all his money at the bookies – I can hardly blame him for taking a punt when he had so little to lose, but a few extra pounds could make so much difference.

The fury mounting inside me needed to be vented. I called Mr Johnson. I told him about David's house and the inhumane conditions he was expected to live in, and asked him why vulnerable and disturbed people were being made to live in one of the roughest estates for miles.

"This really does come as a surprise to me," he calmly said. "I'm unaware of any problems in the area."

"Well if this is such a surprise," I countered, "then why has the last person you put in there returned to the WTRC in fear of her life? She was so intimidated that she didn't even wait long enough to take her belongings with her, and the WTRC has arranged to go and pick them up – which they haven't done yet, by the way."

"No, really, I am unaware of any of this happening," he continued. There is no way that his denial of knowledge could have been true.

I wrote a formal letter to the clinical director, spelling out in detail the filthy, bug-ridden, unhygienic and unkempt state of the house, and the fact that the area was most definitely not a place that was conducive to recovery and rehabilitation. I told him that David was living with me again for the foreseeable future and that although he was prepared to continue with the programme, and with his gardening and the NVQ he had started, we expected him to be placed in a habitable dwelling.

Mr Johnson got back to me on receiving the letter, and told me that David would be able to continue his residential rehabilitation at Stanley House on 14 October, and that they would try to find him another house. He said that I was being unreasonable about the state of the house, and that it was not as bad as I had described. I invited him to go and live there in that case. He did not take me up on the challenge.

* * *

David returned to Stanley House and while he was there completed his NVQ in gardening, which would make it easier for him to find employment after his rehabilitation was completed.

But apart from this positive occurrence, things had not improved at the WTRC during David's time in the house. Karl was sacked, and this

Rehabilitation? **89**

meant that the one ray of light in the centre was effectively switched off. The new carers and coaches no doubt arrived on the job without training and on the lowest wages the centre could get away with (this was before even the first level of minimum wage legislation was introduced, so who knows what they were being paid). David would try to call every day, and if one day it did not look like he was going to call, I would make sure I phoned in and checked up on him. On three occasions he called to tell me that he was hungry, and I had to drive all the way to Stanley House to feed him.

He remained on the £5 a day, and would usually spend it on cigarettes or gamble it away, both no doubt because of the boredom and drudgery of daily life at the centre. Since his accident he had also lost his concept of money and its value, and when he was given any cash he felt he had to spend every penny. This was combined with, or was possibly an effect of, his lack of foresight in many matters that had been a result of his accident. These were aspects of his condition that were specific to him and were not general, so the centre obviously had no way of dealing with them, except to attempt to starve him into realising that money was not a finite resource. If he returned to the centre hungry and asked for food, he would be refused, presumably in the hope that it would suddenly dawn on him that spending his money would result in hunger; it was almost like some experiment with a lab rat, and was immensely discomforting to hear about.

Even though David was clearly not ready for it, another house was found and he was moved into it, all without my being informed. I only found out by chance when I spoke to Mr Johnson after the move. He took the trouble to assure me that this place would meet with my exalted expectations. I was doubtful that David was ready to be independent while his problems with money continued.

On one occasion he had not eaten and spent the day gardening and was terribly tired. He did not have enough money for the bus fare and decided to bet the few pence he had in order to be able to get a bus home. He left the bookies empty-handed, and set out on the long walk home. Towards the end of the walk he was stumbling like a drunk; people were staring and crossing the road to avoid him. He just about made it through

90 *Return from Nowhere*

the front door of his house and collapsed in a heap on the floor and drifted off to sleep. When he awoke it must have been hours later because it had turned dark; he was shivering and in pain all over. He managed to drag himself up the stairs and into his room, where only a light sheet lay on his bed. He pulled it and a bathrobe over his quivering body and curled up into the foetal position and tried to get to sleep.

I phoned the centre as I had not heard from David that day. I was told that he was fine, and that he was either in bed or had gone out (such was the scope of their observation of him). They assured me that he was perfectly well at work that day, and that I should not worry. Some hope of that! I waited for him to call me and the following morning I rang the centre again. What they told made me go cold. Apparently, they did not know where he was, but he would come back when he was hungry, and that would be a lesson to him to stop smoking and gambling all his money away. When I expressed my deep concern at this attitude, they merely told me that David was 'independent living' now, and that he had to learn to look after himself. I was not sure what they meant by this, and made my way straight to the centre. When I got there I had to interrupt a conversation about what the staff were planning to do that night. I asked where David was. I was informed that he was no longer at the centre but had moved into a rented house. I then demanded a key, explaining that I had not been able to contact my son for two days and that I was beside myself with worry.

"No can do," came the response from one of the staff members, who gave me directions to the house then turned to continue the conversation about that night's schedule.

"Excuse me!" I yelled. "Is there anyone who can come with me?"

"No. We're too busy."

"Just give me the key."

"Look," one of them sighed. "We have a key but we don't give them out to people."

"Look, I've driven here all the way from Whitely and I'm not leaving until I know my son is safe. Get me Mr Johnson or Mr Aitken. Now."

As soon as I mentioned these names they handed me the key, and without a word I left the centre and found the house. It did not look

Rehabilitation?

much better than the last place, and after knocking unsuccessfully on the door for a few minutes, I tried the key in the door. It did not work. I banged harder on the door and started to tap firmly on the windows, but I heard no response. A neighbour asked what I was doing, and when he found out who I was said he had not seen David since the previous morning and advised me to try the back door. I could not get past the back gate, which seemed to be jammed with something. The neighbour now seemed quite concerned and offered to call the police, but I had no time to wait and started banging and eventually kicking the door until it opened a little, but even once the lock was broken it still took some force to move as something was preventing it from moving freely. I was relieved to see it was not David, but then set my sights on locating him. Not wishing to startle him, I calmly called his name as I gingerly went from room to room. Even in the cold of the winter there was no discernible heat source, and I could see my breath swirling in front of me. The living room was tiny with old bits of furniture strewn randomly around, and the familiar signs of dampness on the walls. The smells from the kitchen reached me before the depressing sight of black bin bags piled high with half eaten takeaway curry cartons bursting loose. The flex of the fridge was worn – or probably bitten – away and exposed wires glistened in the half light; a sign written above on a piece of cardboard read: WARNING – DO NOT TOUCH – DANGEROUS.

I then made my way upstairs, calling out David's name intermittently, well aware of the danger of making him jump in his condition. I noticed the bathrobe on the bed and in the dim light could just make out the human form beneath it.

"David," I gently said, and to my immense relief, he stirred. "David, why didn't you answer my calls or phone me?" I drew back the bathrobe and looked at his face as he turned to face me. He was emaciated and looked weak; his face had lost all its colour and appeared grey.

With a pitifully weak voice he mumbled, "Mum." But he could not say much more.

"What is wrong, David?" I enquired, sitting on the bed beside him.

"I don't feel well," was all he could manage, as though I could be in any doubt.

I asked him to sit up and told him that once again I was taking him home. He told me he was starving, so we stopped off at a café and I bought him a proper meal, which he could only eat slowly, despite his obvious hunger.

Sadly, David's eating habits are still erratic and he either eats nothing or eats excessively. He was never like that before entering the WTRC and whatever they were attempting to do by withholding food from him has not just failed, but has had a seriously detrimental effect.

* * *

Words cannot express how I felt towards the WTRC at this moment. From the cold, heartless, money-grabbing owner, through the supercilious and deceitful manager and down to the lazy, uncaring and callous coaches and carers, there was no excuse for the way they ran the centre. They saw it as nothing more than a production line, and if there was a way they could save pennies they would try it. The respectability they pushed at potential clients had obviously also fooled the NHS and Social Services; but one seriously doubted if they cared any more, or if they were as obsessed with budgets as the centre itself.

I found out also that Mr Aitken had written to the DVLA in Swansea to apply for the return of David's driving licence now that he was off the medication. The reply letter came to my house, though, and I still have it. I feel sure that Mr Aitken had committed a criminal act here, and one that could have had dire consequences.

I contacted Mr Malcolm, the man from the Shipton Health Authority, and told him that David had left the WTRC in March. Hopefully this would stop the WTRC receiving funds they would have felt were owed to them. He asked me why David had left and I told him it was for his own wellbeing, and then went into all the things that had happened since he entered the centre, and told him I would be submitting a formal report. He pointed out that these were serious allegations, and requested that I come in and see him, which I declined. I do not know if he reported the matter to the local health authority, but I do know that at some point afterwards, the WTRC was eventually struck off the NHS's accredited list.

I started to speak to solicitors and they advised me to build up a case and make a report about all that had happened, but importantly not to enter into any correspondence with anyone involved in David's case, and to keep my cards close to my chest as much as possible. I did think it important that Mr Malcolm knew what was going on, as this was not just my problem but that of many people, so I submitted a basic report to him after having it checked over by legal eyes.

Mr Malcolm informed me that because I had taken David out of the centre of my own accord, David would not be eligible for any further funding at all, not just for the centre. I tried to tell him that it really was not in David's interest to stay there, but he was adamant that the reason was irrelevant and that this was the end of the line, funding-wise.

So for the time being, I was back at square one, looking after my traumatised son with no financial assistance whatsoever.

I made an appointment with Dr Ingalls, the consultant who had originally recommended the WTRC and for whose assistance I was once extremely grateful. She did seem to sympathise with my case, but when I asked her why she had chosen to put David in the WTRC instead of the proven Brain Injury Foundation in Denton, she told me that she saw the former as a new and exciting development in the field, and that if it worked it would prove revolutionary in cases such as my son's. So there we had it. My son and all of the clients at the WTRC were guinea pigs, sent to feed the ego of a doctor and the bank account of his backer with no genuine reason outside the experimental.

Yes, such tests need to be carried out otherwise no new developments would ever emerge, but any sensible person would recognise the parallel need for close monitoring and supervision, external assessment and at the very least the consent of the victims or their families to take part, with the option of withdrawing always open. In this respect, David was failed by the system.

Dr Ingalls ended our meeting by apologising but saying that there was nothing further she could do. The consultant, my GP, the health authority and the centre had all washed their hands of David.

Dr Ingalls was not the independent agent one would have believed she was, I would later find out. It turns out that for a long time she had been campaigning to have a serious brain injury centre in the area. She recognised the need for such a centre and was herself frustrated by the lack of progress. After Dr Bond's resignation, she pounced and took control of The Meadows herself, and even though it was some distance from the area she had deemed lacking in head injury centres, she stopped her campaigning. All along, she had obviously just wanted to control her own rehabilitation unit, and did not care a jot about the Whitely area.

I tried to keep in touch with Dr Ingalls but it soon became obvious that she had heard of my plans to sue the health authority, and could well have been nervous about her own role in the story and her chances of self-incrimination. She must have known that I had letters from her and records of meetings, too. This could have made her decidedly edgy, especially since one of her signed letters stated in black and white that David was brain-damaged at a time when other so-called professionals were denying it.

* * *

I finally got a brief report together to present to the local health authority. The thrust of my report went as follows: the WTRC had claimed that it used highly trained staff when this was not the case. David had to wait for admittance, ostensibly while staff were completing their training but, when questioned, the members of staff admitted that they had received minimal or no training.

Staff were often unavailable and were definitely not on 24-hour watch as advertised. The robberies, burglaries, trespassing, bullying, knife attacks and gun threats attest to this.

Many of the carers themselves suffered from emotional problems, and should therefore not have been in a position to look after others. There was also evidence of friction between staff members, and this was not conducive to the supportive and cooperative community put forward by the centre.

There was little security in place and no protected areas, and security staff were fired for no reason other than to save money; the management knew that there was a risk of intruders, as evidenced by the fact that they asked staff to be vigilant. Soon after security was stepped down, attacks on the premises escalated.

The clinical director had little time to deal with complaints but was a regular contributor to the media. The owner seemed to view the centre as an investment rather than a step towards improving the lives of brain-injured people.

Keith Duke was failed by the centre to the greatest possible extent. He too had been assured that he would be under 24-hour observation, as he was a disturbed individual. He was left alone, his pleas for help were ignored and he was murdered.

Furthermore, Keith Duke's murderer was a dangerous criminal who was taken from remand prison (after being accused of attempted murder) and put right into the midst of disturbed and vulnerable people. Again he was supposed to have been tightly controlled, but almost as soon as he arrived he intimidated the other clients and soon took over and the staff were quite clearly afraid of him. The ultimate act of murder can be blamed on nobody but him, but in allowing a violent person into the centre with the stated belief that he could be rehabilitated, and then leaving him to run amok and take over the centre, the staff, management and most notably the clinical director showed neglect, contempt for the other clients and no small dose of bluster and arrogance over a matter that deserved serious management.

When David had complained to Mr Johnson about the beating up of a fellow client, instead of rushing out to stop it he told David to mind his own business and said that if he took it further nobody would believe him because he was brain-damaged. This was a dereliction of duty to care for the clients.

The flat that David occupied was obscured from view and contained a block of knives, both of which posed potential and easily avoidable risk to David, as well as to previous and subsequent clients. My complaints about these facts were treated as a joke. Shortly after David vacated the flat, it became the scene of a violent robbery.

Several other clients were removed by their families because of security concerns. Some were permanently removed and others only allowed them to stay there during daylight hours. Such was the obvious lack of security and care.

The centre, on the owner's instruction, stopped David's medication for epilepsy despite having no medical authorisation to do so. Any decisions on medication were to be taken by the consultant who first prescribed it or an equivalent consultant who specialised in the area. The chief motivation behind David's medication's being stopped was that the owner wanted David to drive the minibus, which would have been illegal were he to be taking the drugs. The owner actually applied to the DVLA on David's behalf to have his licence returned.

* * *

In isolation, any one of the main points of my case against the WTRC would have been enough to invite serious questions about the centre's fitness to operate. In combination, the picture of neglect, arrogance, unprofessionalism, penny-pinching, exposing clients to danger and simply failing to live up to their stated promises could leave even the most sympathetic observer in no doubt that the centre is not the right place to rehabilitate seriously injured and needy people.

Bearing in mind the financial consequences and the knowledge that I would have to revert to round-the-clock care for my son, my decision to remove him could not possibly have been taken lightly. I put up with much more than many people would have, partly because of my financial situation and partly because there were spells when David seemed to have improved. After all the disappointments, apathy and knock-backs that had been biting chunks out of my fortitude since the day I picked David up from the airport, this really had been my last hope – and everyone I dealt with made sure I knew it.

When today I look at the WTRC's glossy brochure and review the promises that are broken with every sentence, I can do nothing but despair at the wasted time and money that were expended on the establishment. And there on the cover, the strapline that seemed to encapsulate the ethos of the place and offer a rosy picture of care and attention taunts me with its bitter deception. "Making giant steps, a little at a time." The logic of it suddenly crumbles under the weight of the truth. A giant step cannot be subdivided, after all. And the slow, purposeful pace of progress that underpinned the concept behind the centre always lacked the bang demanded by the staff, management and clinicians who were eager for results that would entice new clients. You could hardly call the centre underfunded; but the funding gravitated away from those for whom it was intended and towards the greedy owners and the fame-hungry medics. The slow, methodical modus operandi had nothing to do with making progress and everything to do with making profits.

And what we were left with was people who entered the doors full of hope and left full of despair.

The Western Transitional Rehabilitation Centre
Making giant steps – one forward, two back

7

Out of the quicksand?

After the traumas and upheavals of the past years, David had to undergo a period of psychotherapy for twelve months. There were still traces of hope left in my mind with regard to the treatment he was on. No doubt when the treatment was going well, progress was marked; but so many avoidable external influences kept knocking progress back, and this was painful and frustrating. I would later find out from Mr Johnson that he did wonder if he had been pushing David too hard and making him take on too many responsibilities and face too many pressures too soon. I suppose that with pioneering intervention, the patients also have to be part of that pioneering spirit, so perhaps some failure is to be expected while perfecting the process. But this still does not explain the fact that David's reversals were rarely due to being pushed too hard but rather were more often the direct or indirect result of trying to save money – and to enhance the reputations of the doctors.

Back at home, David had now become frightened and suspicious. It pains me to describe my son like this, but he reminded me of the dogs you see who have been adopted by loving families after undergoing cruel treatment; so used are they to the beatings and torture that they do not seem to accept that they are now in a safe environment, and cower in the corner eyeing everyone suspiciously or defensively. David reacted in this way to kindness and compassion, so it made rebuilding his confidence a tortuous process. It did not help that he would remain silent most of the time, which made conversation impossible, further slowing down the trust-building process. He was so different from the chatty, convivial and popular young man I and all his friends and family members had once known.

His silence was such that he would not even ask to be fed. I would never let him go hungry; but there must have been times when he felt like a snack or a drink, yet not once did he ask. The reluctance to speak about a basic human need made what he did say all the more telling – he pleaded with me not to let him go back to the WTRC. To think that that was his biggest fear, his most pressing human instinct, made me shiver. He vowed to run away should he ever catch wind of an intention on my part to leave him in their care again. I reassured him time and time again that that phase of his life was over, and indeed that I wished it had never begun. I avoided mentioning the place, its vicinity or any of its personnel in David's company.

Like the ice on a pond melting imperceptibly under a winter sun, flickers of personality, trust and – dare I say – happiness began to glimmer through. I had plenty of time to reflect on the mistakes, the bad decisions and an ever-present guilt that I could have done something to save Keith Duke. Often I would get a vision of Keith waving to me in my car mirror as I drove away from him. This was not an abstract thought. It actually happened and was seared into my mind; I do not think I will ever forget him, in his striped tee shirt and blue jeans, waving innocently. It would turn out to be the last time I would see him.

I was through with Dr Barrat by now, and had no trust in him. I decided to register David with my father's GP Dr Dixon, who had always been conscientious and effective. But on our first meeting, when I asked him to sign an exemption form for Council Tax, he refused outright, on the grounds that there was 'nothing wrong with David'. I asked him to get in touch with Dr Ingalls, as she had previously accepted that David had a medical problem; Dr Dixon phoned me later that week saying that Dr Ingalls had not authorised anything. I suspect that this was because now she had possibly caught wind of the fact that I had considered suing them, and 'taking my side' could have made her position difficult. Her refusal to help me signalled yet another dim candle of hope being snuffed out, as she had been one of the more sympathetic people I had dealt with, relatively speaking at least.

Her reaction made me rethink my interpretation of something seemingly trivial that had happened a few months back, during a routine visit to her surgery to have David's blood pressure measured. She had chatted with other people in the waiting room, but then ignored my smile and walked straight past David and me. I had put this down to her not seeing me or being busy, but then we were left till last in the waiting room and were eventually called to see another doctor instead. We happened to leave his room just as Dr Ingalls was leaving hers with her coat on, and again she snubbed us. I had not contemplated it at the time, but it now seemed likely that her betrayal had started much sooner than I had realised.

Mr Malcolm at the Shipton Health Authority had asked me to write a report on the WTRC and I sent it to him. I made sure that he knew not just the bad things that had happened, but also the benefits of the technique when things were going well. I had no idea if my report would have any effect, either in increasing funding of the centre or in tightening up management, but I lived in hope. Benefits that I could list included a reduction in David's aggressive behaviour and an improvement in his hygiene and appearance, which he cared little about before he went there. He was also less self-centred and would offer to help more, and understood the consequences of his actions. And although his memory was still bad, it did appear to have improved. For all the hell the centre had put us through, I was glad of these improvements and rightly or wrongly I attributed them to their work – possibly, I realise, as a means of justification and guilt reduction.

It became obvious over this latest period of caring for David that he functioned much better when he was busy. Yes, he needed frequent rests and he could be distracted, but when his mind was stimulated he was less likely to slip into lethargy. I felt he also lacked contact with other people, especially male contact, and started to wonder if his old employer might have been able to help him out in any way. I approached their personnel manager, Linda, in March to see if it would be possible for David to get his foot back in the door of employment, starting with part-time light duties. I explained all the difficulties, but also that I felt that getting back into this environment would be hugely beneficial to him.

Linda was helpful, but pointed out that there would be several hurdles to leap first; for example his insurance would have to be sorted out, he would have to be passed fit by the company's physician and a whole new contract would need to be drawn up. But she certainly sounded positive about the idea. I am sure that nobody had forgotten about David, and what good company he had been. She told me she would get back to me.

In the meantime, David's brother John and I did all we could to slowly expose David to more stimulation in preparation for him returning to work. I would keep him physically active and John would play games with him in the evenings, and together we would ensure that we ever-so-gently nudged David's tempo up over the days, weeks and months that followed. This was trickier than it sounds, as he still needed plenty of rest and he was not always receptive to or appreciative of our efforts, but most importantly, we knew that pushing him just that little bit too far could be like speeding a car round a corner a fraction faster than its tyres could cope with; we could risk spinning out of control. We were also mindful of the advantageous effect of routine in David's life, which is why change had to be almost imperceptible.

A few months after my enquiry, in September, I received the news that David would be able to start work at his old employer's, although as his old job as a warehouseman was neither available nor within his capabilities, he would be offered a job blowing up footballs (the employer was mainly a healthcare supplier but also had a sports equipment wing). The offer came with the promise that he would be able to take as much rest as he required.

The company was fantastic and welcomed David back with open arms and a generous contract, but unfortunately it soon became clear that the work was beyond him. Despite reducing his official hours to sixteen per week, the job ended up being far too unstimulating and boring, and although the money was welcome, we did not feel the job served David's long-term interests. An important part of his recovery was stimulation, albeit within a controlled environment, so the longer he filled footballs with air, the more deflated he became. We also found it difficult to balance his medication, and even with tweaking and changing the routine slightly we were unable to keep David mentally alert and combat his bouts of tiredness.

The company could not have tried any harder for David, and I am forever in their debt. They bent the rules, kept his job open and basically acted like human beings, a rarity in these times of penny-pinching, complicated employment law and robot-like management.

Finally giving up his job was a bitter mental blow to all of us, but especially David. Because he had never actually been sacked, made redundant or parted company through ill health, he had still technically – and psychologically – been an employee there, albeit on an extremely long period of sick leave. His leaving there signalled a concrete finality, and a sense that there would be no going back. It brought home the arbitrary nature of his affliction. He had become ill on holiday, fully expecting to be back at work in a few weeks, but events had proved this totally wrong.

In a lovely parting gesture, the director called David into his office and presented him with a certificate and a gold pen for ten years' service. David was humbled and surprised, and insisted that he could not accept the gift as his total working time came nowhere near ten years; but the director smiled and pushed his hands back. He offered him a drink and gave him the afternoon off. When David arrived at home he was infectiously pleased; the gift itself was delightful but it was really a permanent reminder of a time when he had been treated with dignity and compassion, and he still counts that pen among his most treasured possessions.

David's return to unemployment also had an immediate impact on me as well as on David. Although I was relatively fit, I couldn't keep up with two young men with bags of energy for long periods. It would be easy for readers to forget that I also had another son, and looking after him, keeping abreast of his schooling, helping his growth into adolescence and keeping on top of simple everyday things meant that I could not rest for a moment. David going back to work, even part-time, had given me the chance to have that moment's rest or even dare to go and have a cup of coffee in town for a change of scenery. Now he was back with me, my old 24-hour routine returned and fatigue began to get the better of me.

Reading a newspaper one afternoon I noticed an advert from the charity Brainstorm asking for volunteers to befriend people with mental health problems to help them avoid isolation, and also simply to have someone to talk to. The idea was that the volunteer would become like a member of the family, with the ultimate aim of preventing the mentally distressed people from becoming outcasts or prisoners in their own homes. This really appealed to me; not only would it give David some companionship; it would also help someone else out.

I got in touch with Brainstorm and we arranged a few days out with other people in similar situations. Although it was a pleasant distraction, however, I soon realised that it might not be in the best interests of either party. We were paired with people who had little in common with David, not just in interests and temperament but also in the degree of their injuries, so one of the two was inevitably always playing catch-up and there was little opportunity to bond. Lucy, who ran the scheme, understood and supported my decision to stop, and thanked me for giving it a try. We remained close friends until I moved out of the area a few years later.

At around this time I had decided to change David's and my GP. I thought it would be a good idea to insist on a female GP, thinking she would be more likely to have a sympathetic ear and less of the macho bluster that I had become accustomed to. I was sure that the male GPs I had dealt with would never have spoken to a man in the way they had spoken to me – although my slight build did conceal one or two surprises if they pushed me too hard.

The community health council gave me a list of names to choose from – two entries long! I decided to try Dr Yvonne Osmond, and arranged to meet her in person rather than just filling in a form or dealing with everything over the phone.

I was quite nervous about meeting her, but as soon as we sat dawn she put my mind at rest. She was definitely a listener and was clearly taking an interest in David's problem. After I had brought her up to date with what had happened (or at least covered some of the main points), she told us that she thought David had a two-minute time span. She revealed that she had some expertise in this area, as she and her husband volunteered to help people with cerebral palsy going to

Lourdes. She assured me that she kept up to date with medical advances and would be able to help.

Dr Osmond was the first doctor I had come across who did not seem to harbour a suspicion that I was the one with a problem rather than David. She also seemed to offer diagnoses herself rather than ask me what I thought was wrong with David, another habit of GPs that I found irritating.

The following months saw a kind of routine settle in. David and I started volunteering at a pet sanctuary as we both loved animals, and although we loved what we did there, we had serious misgivings about the owner. He clearly had something of a drink problem and would often behave inappropriately and unprofessionally, for example allowing new admittances of healthy cats when a cat flu had spread around the sanctuary. We once went to his house with some other volunteers for a social event and I found a magpie in a small cage in his kitchen, squawking in a distressed manner. When challenged, he said it had broken a wing and that it was healing, but I know it doesn't take very long for a bird's wing to heal, and it would still prefer some space in a safe place. Shortly after this incident, we parted company. Admittedly David was beginning to get a little bored with the work, too. The constant hunger for stimulation inevitably goes unfed once routine has set in.

I had by this time decided that it was time to move house. With only the front door between security and a world of pubs, bookmakers and conversations with strangers, just one visit to the bathroom by me could trigger David's wanderlust. Many were the times when I would go upstairs for maybe a minute and come down to find an empty chair where David had been sitting; and most of the time I could not dash out to the street quickly enough to catch him. He could be off for hours. Once he was escorted home in the small hours by police who were following up a burglary, which I hasten to add had nothing to do with David. I had assumed he was in bed at the time. On another occasion he signed up to a life insurance policy sold to him by a door-to-door salesman while I was in another room; I did not find out until his bank account went overdrawn a few months later. The company refused to

Out of the quicksand?

refund us, even though the salesman had obviously taken advantage of David's unnatural trust. Perhaps he was in a state of shock himself at not having the door slammed in his face.

I eventually managed to sell the house and bought a two-bedroom apartment further away. Although it was not perfect – we really needed three bedrooms – it was much more isolated than my old town house, and the nearest shops, pubs and bookies were a fair distance away. I knew David could not walk too far without getting tired, and it seemed to work, keeping him where I knew he was.

The move was accompanied by my finally leaving the care home I was working in too. The ironically uncaring attitude of the management and, I have to say, some of the members of staff there was becoming too distressing. The deciding event was symbolic of the way the place was run. A carer had phoned in sick, but instead of calling in an agency carer to cover, they used a kitchen assistant, while Jenny, the manageress, a nurse qualified in both nursing and residential care had to take over both roles for the night, an impossible stretch of any one person's ability. That night a man called Ronald who had been checked in as a new resident just before my shift, was settling in in the communal room in his dressing gown.

After I had done my rounds and got everyone settled in, I heard a woman shouting from the communal room. I ran in and found Ronald banging his cup on the table repeatedly. He had a distant, unresponsive look on his face and his only sign that I had spoken to him was a slight twitch of the hand. I immediately called Jenny to take a look. She was too busy, she said; and anyway, it was probably his way of protesting about what had apparently been his unwanted admittance into the home. I knew that this was no protestation, but she insisted she was too busy.

I turned back to Ronald and could see that he was trying to say something but could not make his mouth work; the frustration was evident and I did all I could to comfort him. The kitchen assistant and I tried in vain to get Ronald to talk, but the commotion was beginning to stir the other residents, so we had to reassure them and get them back to wherever they had been, all the time keeping an eye on Ronald. Again

I insisted that Jenny come over. She sighed and said she would be over soon. Ronald seemed to calm a little, and eventually my shift ended and I went home.

The next morning I went to work and as I was changing shifts, one of the other carers said to me "Before you go home tonight, make sure there are no dead bodies lying around." Puzzled and, putting it down to the black humour that sometimes creeps into these kinds of places, I carried on with my work; nobody above me had mentioned anything about dead bodies. Of course, I should not have been so dismissive of the comment. Before long Jenny had sought me out and told me the awful news that Ronald had died shortly after I had left; he had been found dead in his chair, merely hours after being admitted, and his body had been sat undiscovered for the whole of the night.

Far from being upset, the care home was in full damage limitation mode, a sense of urgency inspired by the fact that Ronald's distressed daughter was on her way.

The home had a duty to inform relatives as soon as any deaths occurred; sadly, deaths are not uncommon in care homes for the elderly. But shockingly, in this case rigor mortis had set in so even if the home had wanted to lie about the time of death, they could not have done.

When Ronald's daughter found out about what had happened she was furious, and threatened to sue the home. At this point the finger started pointing at me. There were suggestions that Ronald could have died *before* my shift ended, implying that it was somehow my fault, along with that of Jane the kitchen assistant. She threw her hands in the air and vowed never to leave the kitchen again. I was quite sure that Ronald had been alive when I left him, but in any case, I was not a nurse, and I did all I could to get Jenny to come and see to him.

As far as we ever found out, Ronald had had a heart attack, and it might well have proved impossible to save him. But the fact that this care home was woefully understaffed and that unqualified people were drafted in to such a demanding and responsible job was telling. My first-hand experience of care culture went some way towards explaining the treatment David had received – or at least confirmed what I had always suspected.

I had already been seriously considering my ability to continue working in the run-up to Ronald's death. David was becoming ever more frustrated and aggressive towards John, and although he was rarely physically violent, he was constantly threatening. John was living in terror of his own brother and I dreaded leaving them alone together. John was trying to study for his A-Levels at the time, and David's attitude was seriously impacting on his revision. John would end up going over to his friends' houses to study, and this was far from ideal. Often, without John to vent his anger at, David would turn it on me. It is so difficult to continually convince yourself that this was all due to the injury and that you should be compassionate and understanding. His behaviour seemed to defy logic, and his outbursts would seem spontaneous, although in reality it was more like a pan boiling over and blowing the lid off – the result of a continual, rumbling frustration going on in his unstimulated brain.

Because his sense of taste had been damaged, David would demand spicy food as all else tasted bland. I was worried about the health implications, but it was impossible to disagree with David or try to suggest something a little healthier; he would fly off the handle at the mere suggestion of it. He would refuse food, even spicy food, when offered to him; then moments later would start demanding to be fed.

Gambling and money sense remained serious issues. It is impossible to say if he was addicted to gambling or whether it was just a way of killing a few hours and getting a bit of excitement, but the fact that he had no discernible appreciation of the value of money made it hard to believe that winning or losing made all that much difference to him.

So in the end, there was no way I could continue working at the care home. I cannot say I did not enjoy working there when it was going well; I made friends there and the majority of the staff members were conscientious and loving people crushed by an inability to do their job in a truly caring manner thanks to being squeezed from all sides.

* * *

The move into the apartment was a worthwhile experiment but it did not take long to work out that it was far too cramped for a family of three, let alone a family with one easily frustrated and aggressive member. I put it back on the market and started looking for a house, with a very small price tag. The estate agent came up with the perfect article, a run-down three-bedroom detached house on the outskirts of town, right where the green, rolling hills begin to limit the spread of domesticity. It was also quite close to John's friends, which was really useful. I knew there would be work needed to bring the house to habitability, but financially I had no choice, and we moved in within weeks of finding it.

As usual, the first few months in a new location were stimulating for David, and he became calm as he explored his new surroundings. Inevitably, though, once he had become accustomed to it all, the everyday routine started to grind him down. But at least we could all have our own space here.

David's behaviour continued to be troublesome. You could almost call it unpredictable, but really there was a kind of pattern attached to it; almost everything he did could be traced back to his tiny attention span, and if I kept on top of it and stimulated him I could at least know that he would not suddenly snap or disappear. This was hard, endless, work, and there were occasions when it was impossible. One example is the time David and I were queuing up at the check-out in the supermarket, shuffling forwards frustratingly slowly while customers in front fiddled with their change or made small talk with the check-out assistant. Predictably enough, after about a minute, David decided to just walk off outside with some of our unpaid-for shopping. The security staff who came blazing after him wouldn't have known he had decided to pop out for a cigarette; although the shop went into red alert I just about managed to calm the situation down – without even losing my place in the queue! Sadly, though, I heard the woman behind me muttering something along the lines of "they shouldn't be allowed out in public". It was so upsetting to hear people talking like this (and this was certainly not an isolated opinion); I had to bite my tongue to stop myself from entering into a screaming match with her.

David would also get the urge to urinate in the street and sometimes veer off into alleyways and alcoves to relieve himself. I would always insist on him going to the toilet before we went out, and he would insist that he did not need to; five minutes later he would want to. The link

Out of the quicksand?

between hunger and eating was the same. He would turn down my offer of food; then shortly after ask to be fed.

He would also sometimes complain of being hot and strip off in the street, sometimes down to his boxer shorts, and not only in hot weather either – at least once I can remember him stripping when there was snow on the ground.

His most terrifying habit was to try to get out of the car when it was still moving. He had the same cavalier approach to crossing the road, too. There was no stopping, looking and listening, and I can remember vividly his running in front of moving vehicles. He would be so far across that my only possible reaction was to close my eyes to avoid seeing his impending death, but miraculously there would always be a screech of tyres, an angry horn and some cursing from the driver instead. Cursing never sounded as sweet as it did at those moments. He definitely had a morbid curiosity about death, and seemed to be treating life as a challenge, like a video game. I really do not think he was trying to get himself killed when he took such risks, but at the same time I got the impression that death was just one of the hazards of life that had to be confronted, and that one day it might catch up with him.

I once had to physically restrain him from running across the road to punch a woman whom he had seen smacking her child and making her cry. He wanted to show her how she liked it. I suppose his sentiment was admirable – but not lawful – and I am sure the old David would not have reacted in the same way. I wondered if his experiences in the centre had coloured his views on physical intervention – or the lack of it.

A curious effect on David's life was that he seemed to become more attractive to homosexuals, and I would quite often find him in a bar or a betting shop with his arm around a man who was obviously feeling more than chummy with David. For all his problems, he did retain a sparkling sense of humour, and he did love to chat with anyone who would talk to him. I have no idea who would make the first move in these male bonding games, but I do know that he could be tactile and that this could easily be misinterpreted. Keith Duke, for example, who was murdered at Stanley House, had also clearly had affections for David. I am quite sure that David was not homosexual or bisexual, and that there was nothing sexual in his affection; but I can well understand how a gay man would take it if another man put his arm around him. He could just as easily be offended as be attracted, so I had to warn David time and time again about being so touchy-feely. Fortunately neither of us is remotely homophobic, and I could usually make my explanation to both parties understood and take David out of the situation.

This picture of daily life perhaps puts into context the 24-hour job that was looking after David. One of my most powerful fears was who would look after David should anything happen to me. I had several years' experience of his behaviour and along with a mother's intuition I was sure that nobody else would be able to look after him as I could. Although I was far from being able to predict his next move, I had an encyclopaedic knowledge of what would trigger his sudden descents into strange behaviour. Someone starting from scratch would probably not be able to cope, and I feared he would end up back in care or going completely off the rails.

* * *

Throughout the last two years, I had been in regular contact with my solicitor, Elaine Harris, who was trying to establish why the Victoria General Hospital had failed to rehabilitate David after discharge, and why we had been offered no financial help when he clearly needed it (depending on which doctor you spoke to). It was long and painstaking enough just to apply for legal aid, and then Elaine had to try and assemble a case by retrieving medical notes from all the various people and places in whose trust David had been placed. Needless to say, this was a long and tedious process, with zero cooperation from the medical side and maximum pressure from the solicitor.

I was referred to other specialists, but there were always complications. They all seemed to know each other either professionally or with relationships dating back to university days, so the conflicts of interest were obvious. When we tried to find specialists who would represent our side of the argument, the story repeated itself over and over again: a promising independent and compassionate start followed by a sudden reversal such that it would appear that the specialists were fighting against us.

Out of the quicksand?

John sat his A-Levels and his results were disappointing after doing so well in his GCSEs only two years earlier. His teachers expressed their disappointment to me, but I am sure they had no idea how much pressure John had been under.

* * *

Over time, and by talking to and listening to experts on brain injuries, I started to get much better at coping with David's behaviour and personality. For example I learnt that there is really no point in shouting at someone with frontal lobe damage; it will have no effect as this is the part of the brain that would react appropriately to such stimulation. As my own understanding of his condition grew, things did get slightly easier for us all, as much of my own frustrations were really just misunderstandings of his condition. Showing understanding, gently coaxing and using repetition would reap great benefits, and once I made a real effort to try this approach, things definitely got calmer. I took David to the local golf course and spent a whole morning getting him to hit golf balls; then the following morning we went back and did the same thing again. This kind of repetition gradually started to work with him.

Through my solicitor Elaine Harris, an expert panel was assembled to ascertain the exact chain of events from the moment David and John had touched down after their fateful holiday. Elaine herself and I were present, along with two surgeons, a neurologist, a consultant in rehabilitative medicine and a consultant radiologist. They concluded that the consultant surgeon Mr Winner who had made that initial diagnosis had been negligent. Had David been whisked off straight away to start a programme of therapeutic rehabilitation, the panel concluded, his recovery could have been quicker and more certain. Even had this sadly turned out not to be the outcome, it should have been the assumption that that was what was needed; and medical progress was advanced enough at the time to have known this.

This was an exhilarating result for me, which proved what I already knew but also made me frustrated that I could have potentially missed out on so much quality care and financial assistance.

Needless to say, when presented with the conclusion, the same consultant insisted that he had no case to answer, showing that same arrogance to which I had become painfully familiar over the years. To this day he maintains he did nothing wrong, and has made no apology or expression of regret. I accept that mistakes do sometimes happen, especially in such high-stress areas as medicine where wrong decisions can cost lives. If the consultant had come back and said that yes, presented with the evidence that was now available, he might have acted differently, I could have found it in my heart to accept that. But no; this would have represented some sort of failure and could have affected his career.

This consultant, his network of colleagues, university buddies, managers and subordinates closed ranks, denied everything and attempted to cover it all up, arrogantly assuming their defences would never be breached, even if someone did have the temerity to question the diagnosis. When I thought back to all the insults and questions about my own mental health, I almost got angry; but it was too late for all that. Vindication was what I wanted now.

One of the most chilling decisions had been to do nothing with the haemorrhage and to send David back to work in the full knowledge that a second haemorrhage was inevitable and could happen at any time. According to Professor Roberts, this second haemorrhage should not have been allowed to occur. There was never going to be a positive outcome from such an unpredictable event, and all measures necessary should have been put in place to rectify the situation straight away.

My legal team decided that since everything stemmed from the original negligence, the subsequent cases of negligence should not be pursued legally. Although I was upset that so many uncaring people would be let off the hook, on reflection the decision seemed sound, as we could spend years pursuing these individuals and bodies only for them to refer back to the original diagnosis and claim that they were only following it. Rank-closing has its limits, especially when individuals start to have the finger pointed at them.

At long last, the wheels were being put in motion and I had a team of people who were determined to take on the mighty Victoria General Hospital on their own turf.

* * *

Out of the quicksand? **113**

However, just as we were making progress on the legal matters, so David's behaviour was becoming more and more alarming and threatening.

His instincts for his own bodily needs, be they for food, drink or visits to the toilet, were not in sync with his actions. Most disturbing was his relationship with alcohol. He could certainly handle a pint, maybe two, of beer, and I encouraged him to socialise with the few remaining friends he had. They knew the score, and were good friends who watched over him. But David seemed to have no sensation of being tipsy to warn him to stop drinking. He was either sober or drunk. His friends would make sure he did not drink too much, and would lead by example, but he would insist, and then he could become aggressive.

On several occasions I found him stumbling around and reeking of beer. Worse, though, was when he started demanding money from me to buy alcohol. If I refused, he would actually raise his fist and shout "Do you want some of this?" It was devastating. It would end with him storming out of the house and slamming the door, then trying to befriend people at the pub who might buy him a drink, while simultaneously getting aggressive with anyone who looked at him in the wrong way.

I took the story to my GP and she recommended she contact the Brain Injury Foundation (BIF) for me. I was still being effectively punished for taking David out of the WTRC. To the authorities it was my admission that David did not need treatment; the fact that I took him away from there for his own safety would not be entertained. My GP said that it was her responsibility to get David the care he needed and that she would do it. That was heartening. Less than a week later I received a phone call from the BIF, and a few days after that Nigel Williams, a regional assessor, came round and spent some time with David. He was convinced he needed help, and said he would advertise locally for a support worker. I was told by Ali, David's allocated social worker, that I would have to pay, however. I agreed to £21 per month for nine to twelve hours per week. This seemed reasonable, although I had been told by Nigel that twenty hours per week would be required. Despite their good intentions and capable management, the actual support work arranged by the BIF was insufficient. No local people responded to the advertisement, and those who finally came forward were travelling some distance, often from over 40 miles away. Additionally, there was a high turnover of workers, meaning that David could never get to bond with any of them; he felt like a stop-gap for people waiting for other support work to arise. Occasionally someone's car would not start or they were sick, so no assistance would come David's way. In short, it was not working.

There was a growing realisation within the BIF that David was also on the verge of becoming an alcoholic. They recognised an urgent need for proper care to guide him away from this potentially lethal path.

After some confusion as to whether he would be sent to Sheffield, Middlesbrough, or Chester for some residential care, we were eventually told that it would be Chester, and off we went in May.

As before, we found that the people with whom David would be living were in a much worse physical state. Most were wheelchair-bound, and many could only speak slowly and falteringly. We dropped off his belongings in his room and David became visibly upset, tears rolling down his face as he made me promise that he would not be living here forever. Fighting my own tears I gave him my word, and said that he would start to get better now. An assistant arrived and assured me that everything would be fine, and after a hug and a kiss, I left my beloved son weeping, my own tears spilling down my cheeks.

A few days later I got a phone call from BIF. "Where is David?" they asked. When I told them he was in Chester the line went dead for a minute, then the voice on the other end sheepishly admitted that there had been a mistake, and that he should have been in their Middlesbrough centre. I let out a familiar sigh, but there was no point opposing the decision and, as it turned out, I am glad I did not.

A week later I went with him to Middlesbrough. Straight away it became clear that the people here were much more like David: physically able, talkative albeit brain injured and in need of help. Within days of being in Middlesbrough David was giving me encouraging messages. He liked it there, and the people he was with had similar problems and shared experiences to him. He put my mind at rest and for the first time in many months I had a good night's sleep, reassured that David had finally been put in the right place.

Out of the quicksand? **115**

When I went over to Middlesbrough to pay him a visit, my reassurance was strengthened. First of all I could see a real change in David. He seemed more cheerful and relaxed than I had seen him in years, possibly even since he was boarding the plane to go off on that fateful holiday. He showed me round his room, which was in a truly secure block, and the staff there seemed capable, caring and knowledgeable. There was always someone to talk to, whatever the time of day.

David would call me regularly and nothing he ever said dented my conviction that he was being well looked after. My proudest moment was the time he admitted to me that he had a drink problem and that he had joined the Alcoholics Anonymous group. It's a well-known fact that the alcoholic is usually the last person to recognise he has a problem, so just to hear David saying it, and having the strength to admit it to his mother, gave me this heartfelt pride.

I soon started going over to visit him at weekends. I had taken some flexible part-time work in a residential care home so had a little money to take him out for a meal, to go shopping or simply to go for a walk on the beach. I would always take the opportunity to talk to the staff at the centre, and I was never disappointed with the time they gave to me or their conscientiousness. This was definitely no WTRC, the place of David's nightmares which I believed could have potentially ruined his life.

On one visit David told me that some of the residents had had holidays abroad, usually with their families, paid for by the local authorities of their home towns. Far from being some kind of junket, it proved to be hugely beneficial, breaking up the routine and giving them something to look forward to. I contacted Ali, David's social worker, and asked if some funding could be found for a short break away. "Out of the question" was the reply. Ali (despite a distinct lack of qualification in the field of brain injury rehabilitation) deemed it non-beneficial for David to enjoy a holiday, and cut the idea short there and then.

That was when I decided to request that David be assigned a different social worker; Ali had proved ineffective and rather distant on several occasions, and I thought a fresh start was required. But when I spoke to Belinda Clayton, his manager, I was told, in coded form, that should Ali be dropped from David's case it could only be seen as racist, whatever justification I could find of his ineffectiveness. I was not actually being accused of being racist, of course. It was merely being suggested that should this go to a tribunal it would inevitably come up, which I found shocking.

Still, back in Middlesbrough things continued to go well. David's aggression was waning, his drinking was more under control, and he was leading a much more stimulating life. He took it upon himself to arrange to attend meetings at Kickstart UK, a charity that was mainly based in the south of England but had a few northern outposts, which have since ceased to operate, unfortunately, due to lack of funding. They taught David some basic computer skills, but what impressed me the most about the whole experience was that he made his own way on public transport, which served as further proof of how effective his treatment was.

I accepted an invitation from Kickstart UK to go and visit them. It was a humbling experience seeing all these young people, most of whom had suffered some kind of brain injury, tapping away on keyboards doing things I could only dream of doing. One of them even offered to teach me how to use a computer! They were so proud of themselves it was moving.

I met a young man called Andy Reed, whose story had started rather like David's with an accident and brain injury, only Andy's was a car accident. There were massive differences, too, mainly surrounding the fact that he was treated seriously and given all the right care. He was beaming with pride at having just addressed seventy guests at the opening of a vocational rehabilitation centre, something he would never have been able to do months earlier. But his mood turned to sadness when he started talking about his parents. The part of the story about the accident was familiar to me. His mother had helped Andy to recover by devoting herself entirely to his cause. He had been a bright student and had been accepted at university before his accident, and was deciding whether to go on and take the place, albeit a few years later, as it was still open to him. What was giving him doubt was that his mother was beginning to fall apart. His father was looking after her as best he could while remaining at work, but it was as if during the time she was helping her son back to health she was putting the trauma on hold, and that now she was suffering a delayed shock at the accident. He ended up warning me to look out for signs of it happening to me too. This mature, caring and intelligent young man really left an impression on me, and I heeded his words.

* * *

At this point I at last found some hope and happiness after the heartache and the tragedies that had been my constant companions over the past decade. I still frequently wondered not only how much better David's care could have been but also how many other young people had been misdiagnosed, ignored and fobbed off to keep costs low and irritating parents quiet. While every story is different, there seemed to be a convergence in many of the outcomes. Unfortunately, brain-injured people are among the most vulnerable in society and often cannot fight for themselves. And there are unscrupulous decision-makers out there who are more than willing to take advantage of that fact. But at least now I knew that failure was not the only course; successful places run by caring people did exist, although whether you ended up in them was part lottery, part determination.

8

Progress despite frustrations

Progress at BIF was steady and encouraging. The staff understood David's situation perfectly, and were managing to tread carefully the line between over- and under-stimulation, ensuring that David was kept just outside his comfort zone but didn't feel like he had been cut loose. They were like none of the others David had dealt with. They were attentive, transparent and conscientious, always open to my questions and concerns.

I made many trips to Middlesbrough, visiting David and allowing him to show me around. He would take me to the beautiful beach at South Shields, a wonderful place to observe the changing seasons and experience the ebb and flow of the tides. A failing of mine has always been my sense of direction. Once I have turned a few corners in a strange town, I'll need directions to return to base the same day. David's poor sense of direction had been one of the many casualties of his haemorrhage; it had certainly not been inherited – and it had been faultless beforehand. For this reason I was delighted to note that during our many day trips, he would return to his home with a precision that would make a pigeon blush. It was just one manifestation of his progress, and it was joyous to behold.

It seemed at last that all the different channels of assistance were pushing in the right direction, in parallel. David continued to attend Alcoholics Anonymous meetings and he had regular appointments with psychotherapists which, in combination with his positive living environment, were building up in him what most of us take for granted – motivation. Motivation is not just the desire to do difficult things; it is also the spark that makes us carry out everyday tasks, and when that

Progress despite frustrations **119**

spark fails to ignite it is difficult to tackle such tasks, let alone the more strategic decisions we make throughout our lives. Without this spark, it is easy to vegetate on a sofa, acting only when the need becomes too great to ignore, such as extreme hunger. This lack of motivation, closely linked to the reward system of the brain and the ability to see consequences of actions, was behind much of David's behaviour.

David trained himself to be motivated by playing computer games most mornings. It got his brain working and prepared him for the day. He also made sure he wrote down all his plans and appointments, and became punctual and trustworthy as a result. I saw motivation creep back into his life and recognised the resultant will to live overcoming the dangerous apathy that had blighted him for so long.

One difficulty was funding. I found out that other people at BIF who had been having similar treatment for similar conditions were receiving the maximum allowable benefits, whereas David was supposedly only entitled to disability living allowance (DLA), a mid-range benefit intended to help people get by. I was advised to seek a review of his case so that he could be moved up to the full scale, so with the usual number of hurdles to leap, I managed to arrange a visit by a doctor to assess David. I was told not to go along as the staff there would be able to deal with everything and would be present at the examination to answer any questions, but I decided to remain within earshot of the telephone as the medical took place.

When the phone rang, it was Jill, the then manager; she sounded upset. She told me that the doctor had given David short shrift and brushed aside her interjections, going as far as twisting them round to suit his mission: to deny David the benefits to which I and the staff at BIF were sure he was entitled. The reason he gave was that David had improved, which amounted to a change of circumstances which, far from assuring us of an increase in funding, threatened to lessen what he was already getting.

It was infuriating. Even though yes, David had improved, he was still not fully recovered, and might never be. It was like a builder refusing to put a roof on a house because it had improved since being a foundation. More exacerbating was the daily drip of newspaper stories about people claiming DLA and being caught running marathons, playing football and earning money as steeplejacks. It was presumably these cheats who were making the authorities err on the side of caution. Both the newspapers and the public at large treat such criminals with contempt, yet the criminals seem to be the ones who determine the default position of claimants being fit until proven otherwise.

I appealed the decision and was told that the tribunal would be held in Manchester or Middlesbrough. I said I preferred Manchester and asked to be informed of when it was to be so that I could attend. However, it was then held in Middlesbrough and I was completely oblivious of it until I got a letter saying the original decision had been upheld. When I complained, they insisted that if I wanted the tribunal to be re-heard I would have to write to the Secretary of State's office telling them why I failed to attend the missed one. Once I'd done this, the Secretary of State waved it through and the hearing took place in Manchester, with David and me in attendance, and the decision was unanimous: he was entitled to high-rate care and mobility benefit. I was delighted, but that was not the end of the matter. The DLA people appealed *that* decision.

The first scheduled hearing was postponed for several months, and when my case finally went before the board I was allotted a 'troubleshooter', one Mr Simpson, who seemed to be some intermediary tasked with persuading me that I should claim less than I was entitled to and be grateful for it. It was clear that the chair, a supercilious woman called Susan Wilkins, had little intention of accepting that the original decision had been wrong. The hearing got under way and after about fifteen minutes Mr Simpson and I were sent out into the waiting room while the board deliberated. When we got outside of the hearing room, Mr Simpson said he sensed that given the facts, they would probably offer me high-rate care but low-rate mobility allowance, and that I should accept or risk losing both. That's exactly what they offered. I dug my heels in and insisted that David needed help twenty-four hours a day and that it needed to be paid for. Mr Simpson turned to me and said I would be best accepting that I was wrong about mobility and I should take what was on the table, with the possibility of re-claiming at a later date. At first I refused. But Mr Simpson glanced at Ms Wilkins,

Progress despite frustrations **121**

sighed and told me that they could drag this out indefinitely, cancelling hearings and tribunals to their hearts' content until I gave up. This seemed plausible enough, so I accepted their offer with great reluctance.

Ms Wilkins then had me ushered out of the room. Just after I had left, I remembered that we had not discussed back-payments. After all, if David was entitled to maximum care now, he must always have been. I stepped back into the room and Ms Wilkins shouted "Out!" at me, as if I were a child. I said we had not discussed back-payments. She told me that there would be no back-payments, and as I opened my mouth to respond she called security; a burly guard made sure I left for good, but not before I had managed to ask Mr Simpson how he slept at night.

* * *

In September, David came home for five days, timed to coincide with a progress report with the Shipton Health Authority. Our old friend Ali remained his social worker, despite his being useless and often obstructive. He attended the meetings and when he saw David and the progress he had made, he was quick to take any credit he could for it. He informed us of his efforts to gen up on head injuries so that he could help out people like David. I saw it as an attempt to gain favour from the assembled decision-makers. Nevertheless, and thankfully, they did not view David as a completed task to be ticked and signed off, and agreed to continue funding for another year, up to the following September, whereupon he would be moved to independent living at the BIF. The set-up was similar to that at the WTRC, except that the residential flats were located in a single block at the heart of the complex and the individual living bungalows were located on a council estate.

After this positive development, I was able to increase my hours at the nursing agency, bringing in a little more income and improving our family's lifestyle. Things were definitely looking up. Could it last?

The signs did not look good when I next visited David to take him out shopping. On entering his apartment I was hit by a stench, and as I went into the kitchen its source identified itself – days' worth of unwashed pans, cutlery and crockery, a pile of dirty clothes on the floor and grime on the work surface; the general sense of mess continued into every other room. I had let myself in, and when David came to greet me he was wearing filthy jeans, a stained tee-shirt and shoes with no socks. He apologised for the mess and said he had been out with his friends. After a coffee, he said, we would go out. "We're not going anywhere with you dressed like that!" I exclaimed.

This made me dismayed with BIF and I sought an explanation from Ben, his main contact there. He was as open as ever, though, and told me that David was refusing to do any tidying up and that although he had helped a few times, it was not his job, and nor would it help with David's rehabilitation, the sole reason he was there. I could see his point. Ben seemed quite upset by the whole affair; it was as though he had lost a friend, or at least that David no longer wanted to be associated with Ben or the centre. Furthermore, David was apparently getting his money and going straight out to spend it socialising. And worse, he had left Kickstart UK. There had to be some deeper reason for all this, so I spoke heart to heart with David.

Getting to the bottom of things, a picture started to emerge. When David had first arrived at BIF, he was in a similar situation to the other clients, and had plenty of experiences in common with them. But as he made progress, he found himself unable to have meaningful relationships with any of them. He also became a little over-confident, and he could see no reason why he needed to remain institutionalised, even though he still had further to go. In short, his lack of cooperation with the centre and the way he was behaving was a sort of rebellion. He told me he just wanted to come home, 'home' being living with me.

We had a positive conversation and I managed to persuade him that by quitting too soon he risked knocking his progress back. He still needed some sort of stimulation-based routine while his brain sorted itself out; completing the programme now would mean that he would be better sooner. He maturely agreed and vowed to get himself back on track.

I took him to the shops to get some new clothes. This was never a pleasurable experience for either of us; he would rather take anything from the hanger to the counter and get out of the shop as soon as possible than actually try things on, which left him frustrated. When we got back to his flat I cancelled my shift for that night and did a spot of

Progress despite frustrations **123**

washing and ironing for him. When I finally got home I was exhausted, not so much from the running around but from the mental pain of seeing David in such a dishevelled state; this was the last thing I was expecting, particularly after things had been going so smoothly.

After this episode, my regular phone calls suggested things were settling down a little. But the return to routine made David's next revelation all the more surprising; he had found a girlfriend. My emotions were mixed, and would remain so until I had met her. It was lovely to hear at its basic level, another milestone in David's journey to recovery; a chance to have some companionship and the kind of love no one else could offer. But at the back of my mind was more than a niggle. I had seen how easily he made friends and became quite tactile, and while this was not in itself such a bad thing, I had seen how it could lead people to the wrong conclusions. I also worried that this girlfriend might prey on his vulnerabilities, appearing pleasant, but being manipulative or reckless below the radar.

Making sure I didn't seem to be checking up on him, I expressed excitement about meeting this girl, and tried to arrange a meeting with the two of them. David told me that he had asked her to meet me but that she had said that she worried that I would try to split them up or forbid her from seeing him. I found this reaction a little strange, but as I did not know her I resolved to give her the benefit of the doubt. Perhaps she was shy. We finally arranged a meeting at a café, but while David and I were sitting there his phone rang and it was his girlfriend telling him something had come up and that she would not be able to make it.

My curiosity growing, I asked Ben at BIF if he had met her and if so, what she was like. He seemed a little evasive and said, rightly I suppose, that it was none of his business. But this just made me start to worry more, although I did trust Ben enough to know that should David be in any danger he would probably have intervened.

Finally, it was halfway through January and David told me that they were going to have a little trip to Scotland; at this news I had to say that I needed to meet her first. Through David, she said she would like to meet me at my home rather than in Middlesbrough. David suggested they stay over for the weekend. One tidy house later I awaited their arrival. The doorbell rung, I answered it, and there was David, all alone. My heart sank.

"Where is she?" I asked.

"She's bringing in the suitcases!" he smiled. At that moment the door bashed open and two enormous suitcases slid into the hall. Were they planning on staying for a year, I thought. Then I finally got to see her.

Whether I hid my emotions I do not know, but what I saw shocked me. There in front of me was a woman, possibly my own age, wearing jeans, work-boots, a tee-shirt and a waistcoat, with the air, I have to say, of a male about her. She greeted me in her broad Scottish accent, and I snapped out of my staring to say hello.

"Shall I put these upstairs?" she asked. David took over and pulled them upstairs while I went to make coffee. I invited her to sit down and when I returned to the living room she had made herself at home and was slouched in the sofa with her booted feet on the coffee table. And things were about to get worse.

David walked happily into the room and announced that since there was more space in my bedroom, he had put the cases in there. Just as I was nodding cautiously, he then announced that they may as well sleep in my bed too. This was turning into a joke. I took David into the kitchen and asked him, hoping against hope, where his girlfriend was.

"That's her!" he yelped, apparently bemused at my lack of observational skills. "That's Molly." I stared at him for probably a minute, my mouth dry, as I looked for signals that this was a wind-up; I even tried to detect a silent cry for help in his eyes. But he remained nonchalant and looked back at me as though I were an exhibit in an art gallery. Our silence was broken by Molly shouting from the living room: "Hey – shall we go for a pint?"

I shook my head, partly in answer to her question and partly to come to my senses and start taking control of the situation. Who was this woman? David and I stepped back into the living room, and Molly smiled at me before delivering her *coup de grâce*. "Don't worry," she croaked. "Soon you're not going to have to mother David so much. When his compensation comes through I'm going to look after the money and look after David. We've talked about it and it suits us both."

I bet it does, I thought, but this could not go on for a second more.

"What we're going to do is this," I said, as calmly as I could. "You're going to finish that coffee, and then you're going to get your things and leave my house. You are not welcome to stay here."

"Oh, come on" she started, but before she could finish her sentence I took a step towards her and she leapt up and bounded towards the door, then paused. Turning to David she shrugged her shoulders and shouted, "Come on, then! She said we weren't welcome." David started moving towards her.

"YOU are not welcome," I screamed, simultaneously pointing at her and grabbing David.

"I knew you'd be like this," she shouted. "I just knew it. I told you, David." And with that she ran out through the front door. I raced to the doorstep but she was nowhere to be seen.

My heart was beating through my clothes and I turned to look at David. He looked blankly back at me. I could not believe what had just happened, and a shiver went down my spine as I imagined all the manipulative things she must have done to my son in the weeks they had been together. I deduced that she was probably planning to take him up to Scotland for good, living like a parasite on any compensation and benefits that he might be entitled to, no doubt casting him out should they ever cease. The brazen way in which she announced her plans to me made me realise that she had been sure that she was in the right, that she had convinced David too that the plan was sound, and that there was absolutely nothing I could do about it. In her twisted mind, I would just agree with it and just hand David over to her. She probably reasoned that legally I might not have a leg to stand on because David was an adult. But she had not reckoned on the determination of a loving mother to protect her son, whatever his age.

The only satisfaction I allowed myself was that her plan now lay in tatters. She had no doubt been carefully plotting this scheme for months and had probably already spent whatever money she thought was coming her way, at least in her mind.

David spent the next five days at my house. I looked after him and made sure he knew that it was Molly I was angry at, not him. I managed to reassure him that I would love him to have a proper girlfriend and that I was not, contrary to what he believed, trying to keep hold of him and control him for the rest of his life. It did not take much imagination to work out who might have planted that idea in his mind.

The picture that emerged of his time with Molly confirmed my worst fears about the kind of person who might prey on David. Via David's wallet, which was not exactly bulging, she had enjoyed all the trappings of life as a benefit scrounger. Pubs, bookies and takeaway dinners were the order of the day, every day. David's carefully constructed routines were ruined, and it showed.

At the end of the five days I reluctantly took David back to BIF. I knew that restoring his routines and keeping him in touch with the positive people he was associated with up there were what was needed. As we drove to Middlesbrough I made sure he understood that this woman was toxic and that it was Molly who was that problem, not him and not me.

I met Ben and soon got talking about Molly. He confessed that she had actually been employed by BIF as a support worker but that she had not lasted long, being sacked when it became clear that she was getting too close to David. She had also been making him drive her around in her car, which he should not have been doing as he did not have a driving licence. And every day, she would wait until David got his daily allowance and then go to the pubs and bookies to spend it. He ended up effectively moving in with her, showing up at BIF once a day to collect his money. He was also refusing to take his medication. Naturally, this was not acceptable behaviour considering his care was being paid for by the state and he was taking up a placement, so the centre had put in motion plans for his dismissal.

This was all terribly upsetting, but I could not get too angry with Ben because ultimately, beyond physically restraining David, there was little he could do. David was free to come and go as he pleased. I was annoyed that I had not been kept informed about what was going on, though. I could have intervened. And I was particularly irritated because this had all been caused by one of their own members of staff, and that without her employment she would not have had the chance to get under David's skin and start manipulating him.

Progress despite frustrations **127**

I recalled a conversation with David before I had met Molly. He told me that her previous employer had sacked her and that she was suing her manager for sexual harassment. He had got angry just thinking about someone doing such things to Molly and was going to find him and beat him up. I had managed to persuade him not to do it. Apart from the danger he would have been putting himself in, it would probably have destroyed any chances of her tribunal being successful. Of course, this was when I was still under the presumption that she was a decent person. It would not surprise me now if I found out that she had put David up to this act of violence on someone who could have turned out to be innocent anyway.

And so it was that my trip to BIF that day ended up being one of my last. David was not dismissed immediately but stayed there until May, when he came to live with me again. I never bore a grudge towards BIF or any of the people there, although I obviously wished certain things had been done differently. But life is rarely as simple and straightforward as that. Keeping me informed would have been a big step, but apart from that, what could they do to someone who is flatly refusing to cooperate?

Another reason I was not as upset as I might have been was that I believed, as David clearly did also, that his progress had plateaued some time before the recent events. I had not been forced into bringing him home in May; funding was actually secured until September. But for all the amazing progress he had made there, I could sense stagnation setting in. He had expressed his frustration at his lack of like-minded colleagues there, and no doubt the glimmer of excitement offered by Molly was irresistible, misguided though it proved to be.

I cannot emphasise enough that any progress he had made – and it was considerable – was entirely down to the staff at BIF. Their programme for David had proved to be perfectly suited to his situation as it was when he was admitted, but it was threatening to go on past its useful life. Still, I would recommend BIF to anyone in David's position, and I would like to thank them without reservation.

* * *

Unfortunately, the Molly story did not quite end there and then. Presumably doubting my resolve, Molly set about calling me on several occasions with sob stories and faintly aggressive determination to see David. This went on until I threatened to report her to the police. As David opened up about the relationship he did admit to me that he had never really liked her, but that she had had an incredible influence on him and could make him do things against his will. We all know what it is like to be around domineering personalities; it can be difficult to resist their power, although the influence they exercise is usually more benign than that which Molly had on David – and we have thresholds, cut-off points that David was still not fully in control of. It was still a relief to hear him talk about the dynamics of the relationship, though. I did not want him to bear a grudge or think that I was controlling his life, and whom he did and did not associate with (although, of course, I did have to exercise some control over him).

It all went to demonstrate that no matter how much progress David seemed to have made, someone still needed to watch over him. I hoped that a light hand on the tiller would work, gently steering him away from dubious people and situations long before severe evasive action was required; such major upheavals were definitely not what he needed. But as long as he was away from me there would always be that danger. This is usual for people with frontal lobe damage; their own warning signs and brakes are not as clear or as powerful as other people's, and they can be led astray quite easily. It helps potential wrongdoers if they *know* about the condition, which is why, it seemed, he was particularly vulnerable to people charged with looking after the victim. In Molly's case, she took full advantage of this knowledge. Apart from the moral issue of forming a close relationship with someone in one's care, she must have known that what she was attempting was wrong, but went ahead with it nonetheless.

* * *

Little did I know, while all this was going on, that I was about to have a brush with incompetence all of my own. Toothache is one of those pains that are impossible to ignore. Quite why teeth should need a highly sensitive nervous system is beyond me, but I guess we are stuck with the problem; and when you have toothache, it gnashes and gnaws at your every waking hour, these hours being made all the more numerous by the resultant inability to sleep.

I traced this particular pain back to a fragment of filling that had worked its way free, presumably exposing a nerve which reacted every time I took a hot drink. Painkillers were not doing the trick, so I took my problem to the dentist to have it re-filled.

My dentist shook his head after having a poke around my mouth. It was not a filling I required, he informed me; it was a crown. It seemed I had mislaid the healthy sense of medical mistrust I had construed on David's behalf. "Trust me," he said, and I acquiesced.

This single crown was just my dentist's opening gambit. Over the course of the next eighteen months he persuaded me that I needed more crowns, which were becoming as expensive as the ones in the Tower of London. When I returned weeks after having a new one fitted with no discernible benefit, he would convince me that it was because a neighbouring tooth needed one, and once again I would believe him and reach for my cheque book.

But the pain did not go away, unlike the dentist himself, who one day disappeared, leaving his practice partner to fix my problem. Although the last thing I wanted to do was go to that same practice, no other dentist would touch my teeth now as they had been so messed up. The pain was unbearable, like knives slashing my gums and needles being jabbed into my jaw, and through all this I was supposed to be looking after David and John. I had abscesses and infected gums which made eating so painful that I lost two stone, quite an achievement considering I was not exactly large, either in weight or in height. I took so many painkillers that to this day the sight of a white pill makes me retch.

This new dentist started by informing me that his wife was divorcing him. I was not sure why he was telling me this, but I wished him all the best. Looking back, I should have bolted from the room at this revelation, toothache or no toothache. Because one thing divorcees need is money. Solicitors' fees, settlements and child maintenance do not come cheap, and apparently in me he saw gold. I was paying a dentist's practice money to correct botched work that that same practice, albeit a different practitioner, had caused. But I was so desperate that I did not see any other option.

This episode brought home to me the trust we place in people in white coats. It is a strange situation because on the whole they are perfectly qualified and conscientious people, and often they are pushing the boundaries of human knowledge to make life better for everyone. At these boundaries it is regrettable but accepted that errors will be made because they are the zone in which experimentation is going on. But behind the boundaries are the routine practitioners, the dentists and doctors who assure you that they know what they are doing and fill you with confidence which can so easily turn to devastating disappointment. I wonder if it is this spirit of experimentation that has put people in awe of medics while accepting that things do go wrong. In reality, all that is wrong is that some of them dishonestly lure people into their presence with false hopes of salvation, filling their bank accounts with medical fees and research grants. If I were told that there was a fifty per cent chance of a procedure working, I could make an informed decision and if it did not work out, then so be it. Unfortunately many caring professionals have their work put in jeopardy by a few under-trained, over-promising charlatans and plain crooks who seem to have an instinct for seeking out vulnerable people.

The dental story did not end well. I tried to sue the original dentist, but it turned out that I was just one of many, and since he had declared himself bankrupt, there was no chance of seeing him brought to justice. The Medical Defence Dental Board offered me £8,250, which would not come close to paying for the treatment I now needed, but they told me that if I did not accept it I would end up paying solicitors' fees of £7,000. It was a threat designed to prey on normal people for whom that is a great deal of money. Had I had any more fighting spirit left in me, and had I not needed to ensure my sons had a roof over their heads, I might have risked everything and challenged this decision in court. But I simply could not have taken the risk and I accepted the settlement with a heavy heart. The case of the second dentist was treated separately and it was decided that he too had been negligent, and I ended up winning £11,000, which I accepted under the same pressure.

I would later find out that far from living on the streets, my first dentist had simply opened up another practice in the South of England.

Progress despite frustrations　　　　　**131**

Part of my problem was that he had been working without insurance, and he still does. The situation was that should anyone sue him he would simply declare himself bankrupt and move on. It emerged that before he had practised (a rather appropriate word in the circumstances) in the North West he had similarly closed down and left failed surgeries in Scotland and Wales, and no doubt he would continue with his little scheme until the law changed or a disgruntled customer finally caught up with him. If that ever happens, I hope it happens to be Jaws from the James Bond movies, although he'd probably manage to persuade him he could help him – for a price.

I nervously found a new dentist, who showed me X-rays of the dreadful work that had been performed on me. He gave me a tape of relaxing sounds to listen to when I was at home too, a pleasant enough gesture but one which showed a real lack of understanding about the number of opportunities I got to put my feet up and listen to whales and pan pipes. He also recommended another idea, which gave me a start: marijuana! Now I know that the medicinal benefits of this drug are quite widely accepted and there are perfectly respectable campaigning groups trying to have it legalised at least for people with certain conditions, but to have your dentist more or less pass you a spliff is not what you are expect when you are reading the two-year-old *Woman's Weekly* in the waiting room.

I finally managed to get some treatment on the NHS although my NHS dentist expressed disdain for my situation while treating me, which was not the best way to keep a relationship going. After my treatment was finished he struck me off his list for failing to respond within twenty-four hours to a letter.

* * *

So here I was, with David back with me, a couple of years of stress behind me, and a new and real sense of optimism.

9

The carer's tale

I would like to describe the following weeks as a period of calm; but they were far from it. Nor were they a time of reflection. When David came back to live with us, my days were spent looking after him, albeit nowhere near as intensely as when he was at his worst, and my nights, or whenever I had the house to myself, sparked off a continual round of introspection, self-questioning and attempting to make sense of the previous years. Occasionally this would become almost trance-like, and I felt as though I was having out-of-body experiences. I am sure that this was all down to fatigue. Not only was my daily life hard work physically and emotionally; my sleep patterns had long since been shredded by worry and exertion. I felt like a puppet, being taken from scene to scene with little power to intervene.

Little things would pop into my mind, which at the time had seemed almost meaningless but in my new state of mind seemed to have immense meaning that was just out of my grasp. I struggled to make sense of things that *really did* have little meaning, a frustrating experience. Some recollections, however, would have made more sense fast forwarded to another point in time. I relived all my missed opportunities to put David on a better track and could usually pinpoint the exact moment when the fork in the road led me the wrong way. The idea that I had the mighty tool of hindsight at my disposal did not seem all that significant to me. I was suffering from guilt, and other people's decisions and actions still managed to be my fault, even though in reality there were often few alternative routes I could have taken.

What I was really going over was my journey from utter naïvety to becoming the kind of lay expert any close relative becomes when

The carer's tale

confronted with a serious condition and a mistrust of the powers that be.

I feel I need to say that the majority of those working in the health service are not bad, self-serving people. There are those in every pay scale, from care home staff to regional managers, who will indulge any opportunity to aggrandise their image or make a quick buck, but they are relatively few, despite my anecdotal evidence. There are systemic failures caused by the way the health service is arranged, but I dare say they happen all over the world. On the whole, health workers do an incredibly difficult job miraculously well, often for little reward. But my own dealings with people who were sure to put David on the road to recovery rather than line their pockets or take advantage of him were thin on the ground.

Apart from the welfare of my sons, something else drives me forward in my terrier-like quest to right the wrongs that had filled my past. I want to make sure that nobody else has to go through all the torment, jump through all the hoops and take such enormous risks to ensure the best possible care for a loved one. This sentiment is a common theme among those who have been affected by a preventable trauma. Often, they are also mourning a loss. In this respect I was lucky. I realise there were plenty of occasions when David could have been killed, when the people who were in charge of his care had had their minds on other things.

The nagging in my head has never really gone away, but I hope that making the story public will have a cathartic effect. Even though I could not stand paperwork, filing or even using email or the internet, and would much rather have been dusting the top of the living room cabinet, I had to write this book. I plan to ceremonially burn my collection of press cuttings, official letters, diaries and items of research once I am satisfied that they can serve no further purpose. OK, most of them, anyway.

In hindsight I think, although there has never been any such diagnosis or test, that I was developing a sense of paranoia. I was *convinced* the whole medical establishment was out to get me. In my mind I had somehow offended someone and word had spread that I needed to be stopped. In the relative clarity of the present day I can see that this is fanciful, but immersed in the drudgery and pain of the time, it was the most logical and sensible explanation. I trusted no one, and it is possible that I mistrusted people who would in fact have been able to offer something positive; I shall never know. But suffice it to say that there were times when I truly thought I was in danger of being bumped off. I would look over my shoulder and see people who I was convinced were concealing a weapon and waiting for me to leave the busy streets.

The whole experience has also changed me considerably as a person. I hope I was never prejudiced or bigoted in any way, but I did see people in polarised terms when it came to their wellbeing. I blamed people for their conditions of self-neglect or lack of willpower, convinced I was right when it came to health. For example I would have had little sympathy for an alcoholic before all this happened. But many were the times when I wondered if I could have used alcohol to blot out the pain I was in. The temptation was certainly there, and it sat on one side of the see-saw, with responsibility on the other. It would only have taken a slight loss of self-confidence to set in train a descent into oblivion, and it did not seem a bad idea. Luckily I never did make that descent. I made sure I never kept alcohol in the house so I had to physically go out and get some when I wanted it, which served as a cooling-down period. It worked. But it did not stop me lying in bed and wishing I never had to get up again.

Anyway, dealing with David banished the potentially prejudiced part of me to history. There are always underlying reasons, usually hidden, often undiscoverable, why people take a certain route through life. This route may not be their own choice or, if they did choose it, the thought process that led them to it could well be unreliable. I can imagine how if in the old days I had seen a man behaving aggressively in the street, I would have tutted, crossed over and been grateful that he was not part of my life. But my son David became that man, and his ire was triggered by the sight of a fellow human being mistreated. Of course, we cannot analyse every situation life throws at us. There may even come a time when I recognise what leads health professionals to their selfish and dangerous actions. Maybe.

In due course I got myself a job at a supermarket check-out. I thought I was ready to start being normal again after sixteen years as a punchbag dodging the rain of jabs and hooks. I yearned to go shopping, earn some money, catch up on the TV and news, have friends round or pop out for a drink every now and again. But even that job, which is supposed to be relatively simple, was beyond me. The main reason was my lack of concentration. Every time I stopped thinking about passing the products over the scanner for a second I would lose my train of thought. Unfortunately, people are just too friendly and willing to start up a conversation. Maybe I looked sad or worried and they just wanted to cheer me up; or they might have been lonely themselves and looked forward to these moments of social interaction. Whatever the reason, all it took was a courteous greeting or an inquiry and I would have to psych myself up again to get started or completely lose the plot.

It was during this time that I first got the idea to start writing down my experiences. I realised that if I died this story would go untold. The people who destroyed my life would go on climbing the career ladder (I know they probably still will) and the institutions that so many people put their trust in, but which proved to be criminally irresponsible, would never be shown up for what they are. Once I started writing, it was difficult to stop. I would pour words out onto the computer screen until I was left with monumental blocks of black on white without so much as a paragraph break in them. If I could have set up a tube from a tea machine to my mouth I would have done so. I had lost so many ideas that I worried about being disturbed.

Then after a chapter was finished the urge would stop. I would feel an immense sense of relief and inner calm; I could relax and be constructive. It felt like those penny-falls machines in amusement arcades. Every now and again there would be a great landslide and a satisfying jingle of copper against steel; but it was only ever a temporary sensation. Over the coming weeks the pennies would start to overhang the precipice, urging me to start feeding the machine again. I would boot up the computer and start to compose another chapter, each new recollection inspiring many more which I had to put onto the page before they evaporated forever. Most of us are unlucky enough to experience traumas. When they go on for some time, they have a wearying effect. When we are tired, we get a fuzzy feeling, our senses lose their sharpness and we need to go to sleep. When we're more deprived of sleep than usual, for example as parents of newborns or frequent long-distance flyers, we need several nights' rest or a bit of catching up. But the fatigue I was suffering from was not curable by a few early nights, even though at first I deluded myself that it was. I was dragged down by the continual stress, worry and fear that had blighted me for well over a decade. It was only now that I realised just how tired I was. It was a deep fatigue, impossible to budge, and the idea that I might one day see as clearly as I used to seemed as unreachable as a distant star.

I realised that I had been living on adrenaline throughout the trauma, and that now my body was reacclimatising to normality, the supply had been shut down and I was on my own again. It was a sobering thought.

Knowing that you need to keep going is most important. In time, the fatigue will start to recede, but you need to be patient – keep active, socialise and do enjoyable things even when your body is crying out for soft, warm blankets. I found gentle exercise helped greatly and didn't want to be pushed faster than I felt comfortable with. Another solution was talking. While this book was cathartic, it was no replacement for being able to talk to someone with an open mind. I have been lucky to have friends, family and eventually a loving partner to confide in. There really is a psychological benefit to unburdening yourself and sitting next to someone who clearly feels your pain; it is reassuring to see them nod, grimace or laugh at the right moments as it shows that your own feelings are not as irrational as you sometimes fear.

So while I can happily report that there is hope for the loved ones and carers, it is a battle that has to be fought head on but with sensitivity and self-knowledge that may need to be acquired the hard way.

* * *

Over the course of the previous years, including when David was in Middlesbrough, I had to battle with another problem, one which affects many people, mainly women, and one which is often wrongly put down to people being image-conscious.

Reading women's magazines, anyone would think we are all obsessed with our weight, and on a constant mission to drop a dress size. But the weight loss that the magazines lightheartedly cover is nothing like that caused by ongoing stress that is not healthy and is not attractive. When I first shed a few pounds, people would comment, and I would take it as approval. But then I noticed not a weight loss, but a weight gain. Whether it was because of the seemingly neverending trips to solicitors or the stress of never knowing what my tomorrows would bring, I realised that I had put on a pound or two. Anyone who had not seen me for a few months might have noticed, but I didn't notice until one day I caught the light from a different angle.

The worry of not being able to claim any kind of benefits for David haunted me day and night. There was no way he would cope if thrown back into the jobs market and although we were coping – just – by scrimping, borrowing and claiming the pittance that we could, I knew that should anything happen to me, David would fall prey to all manner of vultures, public and private. His brother John, who was just starting out as an adult and turning out to be a responsible, caring and mature one, would have to pick up the shield and the lance. It simply would not have been fair on him to have to spend his youth like this, even though I know he would gladly have done it. So permanently securing assistance for David was my life's mission. And the stress made me neglect my own health and welfare.

I had become something of a grabber and a grazer. I had so many appointments and such a disjointed, random pattern of life that I would just eat something because I thought I had to. If I had a meeting at midday I would have my lunch at eleven o'clock knowing that I might not be available to eat again until two or three in the afternoon. By then I would be hungry again and would eat again. Looking after David also left me little opportunity to have a three-meal-a-day routine, so I ate the wrong things at the wrong times. It might have been keeping me going, but it was storing up problems. Looking back I probably was not even particularly large. I just felt it.

So on that fateful day when it dawned on me that I had piled on the pounds, I resolved straight away to cut down. And although my willpower stopped short of my nicotine addiction, I found giving up food incredibly easy. I allowed myself to have as much coffee as I desired as long as I only ate about half of what I would normally have eaten. My body reacted by eating itself and the bits of me that I had found so awful started to sink back. I reached the point where I would not feel hungry, and this pleased me. I would sometimes think about eating and tell myself that that would just be eating for eating's sake.

My mother was the first to notice and point out that I had lost weight. She was not praising me but warning me. However, my blinkered self did not hear it that way. She tried to seek reassurance that I would not go too far and I laughingly made a joke about loving food too much for that to happen, even though I felt like I could do without it. My size 12 clothes started to feel loose and the dress-making industry rubbed its hands together.

In fact, I had become the very definition of an anorexic. I would look in the mirror and see a fat person, even when my clothes were hanging off me. There was the evidence: the clothes that fitted me neatly several weeks ago, the trousers that used to fit well without a belt, were now loose on me. Friends and relatives made worried comments which I would brush aside. Intellectually I was aware that I must be losing weight, but I still saw a large woman in the mirror and was quite comfortable with the idea that I could lose a few pounds. I went shopping for clothes with my sister after every item in my wardrobe became unwearable. She took me to a place that specialised in fashion for petite women. The size 8 range was way too big; the size 6 range had no structure on my frame; and ... well, that was as petite a woman as they considered it worthwhile manufacturing clothes for.

But still, when I weighed myself and the gauge refused to move past 6½ stone, I was not alarmed; I was happy. I probably only started to worry when I reached 6 stone and when I had to sleep on top of my duvet because lying on the mattress on its own hurt my bones too much.

Then, I got so low that I became convinced of my own imminent demise and decided to visit David before I died. At the time it did not seem like my cleverest decision. With no fat under my skin to protect my bones and my nerves from the world, even the tiniest brush against any object would make me wince. Still, I decided to drive the 130 miles

The carer's tale

139

to Middlesbrough. I figured I would be fine if I just sat on the motorway going in a straight line, stopping for a rest at every service station.

I eased myself painfully into the car, where I found that even changing gear caused my hand agony. Still, I thought, on the motorway I would not be changing gear all that often, and I carried on. I counted down the miles to the first service station; already I was tired out. I managed to make it there and could barely walk from the car to the building. I stood staring at the food available for minutes; none of it looked remotely edible and some, such as sandwiches, would have inevitably stuck in my throat. As I pondered the products on offer I was oblivious to the queue building up behind me and the staff urging me to choose something. I waved the customers through apologetically and when I eventually got to the counter the woman working there thought I was joking when I asked for two small sausages and six chips. I took the plate to a table and just sat staring at it. Two chipolatas and six chips look like a mediaeval feast when you are repulsed by the mere idea of food. I got up and bought a pint of milk, then returned to my meal. It seemed to make sense: a sip, a bite, a sip, a bite. Indeed it worked up to a point.

An hour later, filled with embarrassment and self-loathing, I considered my meal finished as I had eaten some of it at least. I stood up, was overcome with nausea, ran into the toilets and threw it all back up.

Back in my car I continued along the motorway. With all the stops it took me eight hours to cover this 130-mile journey – that's 16 miles per hour. But at least I had made it. I had not told David that I was coming as I was not sure I would make it, so when I turned up, and he happened to be at reception talking to Ben, they both looked at me in utter disbelief. Of course, what they could not believe was not so much my presence, but my lack of it. There was nothing of me, and looking at David gave me a clue as to what he must have seen in my face when I first met him at the airport years before.

I had planned to go home that night after a short visit, but it was getting dark already and I was exhausted. Ben and David insisted I was going nowhere, and offered me the visitors' room for the night. I accepted gratefully. David suggested we go out for a meal, which of course this was out of the question for me. But I said I would accompany him and he told me he knew a Chinese restaurant nearby; we got there just as they were opening and we sat and sipped a drink while they prepared our table.

"What do you want?" he asked.

"Nothing," I replied. "I've eaten." I was referring to the milk, which was currently swilling down a drain pipe somewhere.

"Well I'm not eating if you're not," he said, shuffling to get his coat.

"Order me something. I'll see if I can eat it. No starter for me though."

David scanned the menu and ordered himself a chicken curry and me a chicken omelette. With the restaurant slowly filling with customers and the atmosphere becoming more convivial, we sat awkwardly together while he ate his prawn starter; all I could think about was what I would do when my main course arrived. When it landed on the table, I proceeded to mime the act of chewing while I toyed with the food, trying to put it in some three-dimensional arrangement that would look like I had eaten half of it. David wolfed his meal down then looked over at my plate.

"You've not touched it," he said.

"I have," I lied.

"Well," he sighed, sitting back in his chair, "we're not leaving until you've eaten it." He may have remembered himself as a toddler being unable to go out to play until he had eaten all of his liver and cauliflower. The tables had turned.

I tried to explain that I had no appetite, but he was having none of it. The restaurant reached its busiest time and then gradually people started drifting out until, just like when we had arrived, we were the only ones there. The staff hovered, clearly wanting to go home, but were too polite to move us on.

But amazingly, slowly and painfully thanks to my now-tiny stomach, I managed to eat three-quarters of my chicken omelette. It was a turning point because I would not have thought it possible. I would definitely have stopped long ago ordinarily. But I was with David, who had recognised that I needed feeding and insisted that I eat. In itself this was the sure sign of a loving son, but in context, with his restless

The carer's tale **141**

nature tugging at him to get up and go with every tiny slice of egg that I was preparing, it was a massive gesture.

I thanked the staff for their patience and we made our way home. When I woke up the next morning at ten o'clock I could not so much as remember going to bed. I was out for the count and had the longest, deepest sleep I could remember having for some time.

I asked if we could go for a walk on the beach if possible. It was a bracing day and when the fresh air hit my face I was filled with vigour. Out of nowhere I asked where we should go for breakfast. David suggested a beach café and off we went, sat down and ordered two breakfasts, and I ate most of mine.

We visited a smuggler's cove and a natural wonder where thousands of sea birds nested on a cliff face. Again, this built up my appetite so we went to a pub-cum-restaurant heaving with tourists and ordered food. I also managed to have a supernatural experience. I saw a black and white cat darting between the chairs but David claimed he had not seen it. The waitress told me a story of a ghost cat that was supposed to live in the pub, a favourite haunt of the smugglers. It certainly made me question my natural scepticism about all things supernatural, but maybe they were spinning a yarn to the gullible tourists. I would certainly like to think that cats live forever in spirit, especially considering what was soon to happen to my own beloved pet.

Back at the foundation I said my thanks and goodbyes, feeling guilty about putting David through this. I was supposed to be looking after him – not the other way round. But by gently forcing me (I can't think of a better way of putting it) to eat that chicken omelette, he had quite possibly saved my life, because for the first time in months I had discovered an appetite. My attempt to eat in the service station was the lowest point of my anorexia, but after that it was up all the way to my natural weight, where I stopped, and remain to this day. Nowadays, the tendency is to go to the other extreme, and it is a constant battle not to overeat.

Whether it was looking into the eyes of my son that saved me or his determination not to see his mother tumble into an abyss – or a melding of the two – I do not know. But whatever happened in that

Chinese restaurant worked, and I wish all anorexia sufferers would experience just one such epiphany.

That weekend John came home from university, as he did every other weekend. He would never stoop to lecturing or haranguing me, but he had repeatedly made it clear that he was concerned about my weight loss and that I needed help. As usual, he walked through the door and I saw the look of pain on his face when he saw his emaciated mum. But this time I stood up, gave him a hug and said, "It's going to be all right now. It's over."

I really felt for John because in many ways he was the forgotten victim of all this. He rarely received the support and sympathy that was owed to him because he was not the actual victim or the one directly caring for him. But he had suffered untold stress over the years. From the initial discovery of his broken brother, through the operations, being the subject of violent threats and intimidation, the resultant dip in his school performance and then to see his mother fall apart, it was more than most people have to put up with throughout their entire lives. But he coped admirably, and worked his socks off to get into university. Although I could never devote as much time to him as to his older brother, he pulled through and there was nothing I wanted more than for him to get his degree. Sadly, when David returned home, John gave up his studies mid-term to help us. He vowed, however, he would continue with his degree one day.

* * *

Events that would have been distressing in isolation took on greater significance now that I had become so weak. Within weeks of each other I lost both my cat, Suki, who had lived sixteen years and who had been my soft and friendly companion for all but her first six weeks, and my dear old King Charles Cavalier Spaniel, Zoë. The poor dog had been brought to me by a passer-by who had found her being savaged by a neighbour's dog which was always left to roam the streets. It had already bitten a child some weeks back, but its attack on my dog was particularly bloodthirsty. I thought Zoë was dead when I saw her because one of her eyes was hanging out of its socket by a thread, and she was motionless. But when she saw me with her good eye she leapt up

The carer's tale   **143**

to greet me. I hurried her to the emergency vet, a half-hour drive, where she was patched up as well as could be expected, but it was clear she did not have long left. After this I got the police and solicitors involved and in culmination my neighbour paid me a small amount of compensation which just covered the vet's bill, but not the solicitors' fees.

Again, though, this event left me blaming nobody but myself. I scolded myself for 'neglecting' my dog and cat while I was looking after David.

* * *

During one of my reflective periods, I recalled a man with whom, years before David's accident, I had struck up a friendship. He had been going through a very tough time looking after his wife who had been suffering greatly from ill-health and I remember him saying that he did not have a life apart from his work and his duties to her. The statement resonated down the years and I took it upon myself to call him, partly seeking a sympathetic ear, partly wishing to be one.

When I called he remembered me and was pleased to hear from me. His wife had now developed cancer and it was spreading around her body, but the work he had thrown himself into was proving fruitful and he had become quite wealthy. We arranged a quiet drink which turned into a meal, and as soon as we sat down at the table I poured my heart out to him and listened to his own heartbreaking story. I certainly felt better after this, and assumed he did too as we soon struck up a real friendship and used to meet from time to time to talk over our problems. We were able to get our latest frustrations off our chests and then relax and let the conversation take all sorts of meandering routes that had nothing to do with our problems. It was just what I needed.

Inevitably, the friendship got stronger and turned into what I could describe as a close though not physical relationship. He seemed like such a good listener and affected me so positively that I would sometimes refer to him as my knight in shining armour.

But our friendship was to take a turn for the worse. As his poor wife's cancer got worse and spread further, it had made his own commitment to her higher and the emotional strain much more intense. This meant that the balance of unburdening was in his favour. He got the impression that I was only happy when I was the one opening up, and thought that now his problems were greater than mine, I was somehow unhappy with the relationship. I know that this was not true; I was grateful to him for listening to me and now that his needs were increased, I was happy to do my bit. We talked it through but I do not think he was convinced. Then sadly, his wife died.

My friend now started to call me more often to arrange drinks and meals out. At first I tried my best to always say yes, because he was grieving and I knew I could help him. But it got to the point where his invites became so frequent that I had to ask him to slow down. Whereas he was now free to do whatever he wanted, I was still exactly where I always had been, and there was only so much time I could devote to him.

Our friendship collapsed, with him feeling at first resentment and then something approaching hatred. While I tried to understand him— I had, after all, experienced some paranoid feelings and mistrust of people myself – he made the friendship irrecoverable by belittling and humiliating me. Only then did I realise how much I was relying on his friendship and wise words; when he turned against me I fell flat on my face, completely unsupported. He was by now a successful businessman and had a villa in Spain with its own swimming pool, which he had offered to sweep me away to as soon as I got my passport. But of course this was out of the question, and he must have known it.

I had unwittingly stumbled into a relationship perhaps always intended to be more than just talking. He probably wanted me as a lover, and I think my obvious rejection led him to turn on me. As a company director he was used to getting his own way, and the vitriol he poured on me when I did not let him get his way was painful and severe. I cannot deny that our time together had at the time seemed worthwhile. It did make me feel good and brought me out of my shell for the first time in years. Flattery is a powerful thing.

What he never knew was that the manner in which he let me down made me much stronger than I had been previously. He gave me my spine back and made me the fighter I remain to this day. I do believe that things happen for a reason. My friend, whom I recognised even at the time as having little in common with me, helped me through the lowest days and inadvertently thrust me into the real world as a stronger person.

The episode also taught me that while it is fine to share problems with friends and to build up support networks, it is probably not such a good idea to base a relationship on pain or grief. Sooner or later one of those involved will have a life-changing event and the relationship will become baseless. And it certainly does not make sense to use a relationship as a means of counselling. That is something that is best left to professionals. Dispassionate as they are in a way, they know how to coax out of those they are counselling just as much as the latter is comfortable with.

* * *

Needing money and with an overdraft that makes graduates look like they were not trying hard enough, I decided to try and enter the job market once again. I applied for agency work as this would be more likely to produce night shifts, which would have been better to accommodate my daytime dealings. The agency dealt with medical staff and they offered training; I thought this would be a good way to get into some kind of nursing work. Despite being perilously underweight and shaking through the interview with stress and weakness, I was offered some work. I think the fact that I offered to work nights helped my cause; this is clearly the least popular shift. But what I did not know was that night work actually paid more money, so I was more than happy to accept.

I was really thrown in at the deep end, or so I thought, as my first work was in a hospital, Brookside General. I can remember being shown around my ward by a nurse; she quickly showed me where the toilets were and all the other things patients were likely to need. I said I was concerned that I could not take it all in, but she told me not to worry. Then I found out I was also expected to take patients' blood pressure and temperature. I really started to panic now and the nurse's assurances that I would know it all by the end of the shift hardly put my mind at rest; I also pitied my first few patients! She informed me that I would have to learn quickly as they were short-staffed that night, which probably explained my swift employment; it certainly was not for my experience.

146   *Return from Nowhere*

I just remember standing at the end of the ward and looking down at the rows of beds whose every occupant was looking back at me. They had no doubt heard my protests and were probably worried about where I was going to stick the thermometer. Then one of them smiled at me and said, "It's not the end of the world," which made me relax a little.

The nurse and I took sides of the ward; she took the left and I took the right. I made a nervous start of putting on the blood pressure armband, and the machine started to pump it up. I watched as it got bigger and bigger and then, with an enormous pop, tore off the man's arm and flew onto the bed. At first I was mortified, but then I noticed the man in the next bed had started chuckling and then giggling uncontrollably, and within seconds the whole room was in laughter, the only complaints coming from the ones whose guffawing was hurting their stitches. When things had calmed down I noticed one man was jabbing his finger across the room, pointing at another patient. I twisted round and saw a red-faced man lying there with thermometer in his mouth that I had placed there five minutes earlier. I could have sworn I had taken it out!

This all lightened the mood and by the time I was leaving the room everyone was talking to each other and I had become an instant expert at taking blood pressures. The nurse asked me how I was doing, and one of the patients shouted "Marvellous!"

This reaction blew away all my fears and inhibitions. They were just people, after all. I am sure most of them would rather be somewhere else, and anything that injected a bit of jollity into their long nights must have been a relief for them. No doubt every one of them had had a first day in a job, and we all know how weird and intense it can feel. But overall, they recognised me as someone who was there to help them, and I think people will always appreciate that. Yes, there are some awkward patients but they are in the minority.

I loved chatting to the patients, and I hope they felt the same way. Occasionally I would talk to cheerful, friendly people who, it would turn out, had problems that dwarfed my own. It helped me to gain a sense of perspective and their strength and positive attitude made me feel better about myself.

Another welcome effect of my work was that as soon as I got home

The carer's tale **147**

I would have a slice of toast and fall asleep, and stay soundly asleep for hours – something that never used to happen.

I started to consider myself valued by the nursing staff, which boosted me no end. I seemed to cope with stressful situations better than others did, and was gradually allocated the more demanding wards. I think that the job kept my mind off my problems at home, and so it followed that the more that happened on the ward, the more absorbed my mind would be and the less time I had to fret about my own life. I was pretty good at flicking off the job switch when I was not actually there. It may sound callous, especially after dealing with some hopeless and distressing situations, but I would barely think about work once I had clocked off. This attitude is probably not all that uncommon – indeed it might be a necessity – in the medical professions.

Little did I know at the time that I was being taken advantage of, just like many other agency nursing staff. When you are new to an agency you are eager to please, so if they offer you a shift, it is difficult to say no. You imagine yourself being dropped from their books for the mere audacity. This led to occasions when they would ask me to do two shifts in a day, for example, effectively a sixteen-hour day, sometimes in hospitals miles apart. What I did not know was that we were actually in the powerful position, as there was a lack of agency workers and we could have raised our value had we known. The more experienced agency workers did know, and along with the supervisors would work the newcomers to the bone so they could have an easy life. Staff turnover was very high. I realised after a few weeks that I rarely saw the same people more than two or three times. At first I imagined it was down to shift patterns being out of sync with each other or there being so many of us that we would be in different wards all the time, but no – it was people starting, coping for a few days or weeks and then burning out.

There was a way they would ask you to work extra shifts that was so formulaic that it must have been standard procedure. First they would politely ask if you could manage another shift, as though they were friends asking if you wanted to go for a drink. If you refused, they would plead with you or put pressure on you, saying they were short-staffed or similar. And finally, if that did not work, the mood would turn ugly and they could be angry or threatening.

I learnt to stick up for myself and only do one shift a day and also to make sure it was the same shift to keep my body clock ticking. After a while you could almost be guaranteed those hours and they would stop putting pressure on you when they learnt that you were no pushover. It was a learning process, but it worked.

* * *

The trials of those caring for loved ones are recognised but rarely addressed. In many cases (although I am not claiming it to be the case in mine) the one doing the caring is the one suffering the most, because as well as the troubling experience of watching a loved one decline, often terminally, they lose their own life and the things that kept them comfortable are no longer available to them. Fatigue, greater than anything that it is possible to prepare for, will creep up, and with no prospect of a rest in sight it can feel as though the walls are closing in.

There can be hope, and things can get better, but from one day to the next this is hard to see. In such a state of mind it is possible to become vulnerable to other people, to illness and also to oneself. I consider myself lucky to have emerged into the daylight in more or less one piece, but I am probably not typical in that respect. Although it feels simply wrong to claim victimhood when it is another person who is the 'real' victim, it is a fact, and it is best confronted by all carers.

10

Operation NHS

During my time at the nursing agency it dawned on me that I might actually come face to face with Mr Winner (the neurosurgeon who we had last seen about eight years ago) in my daily work. For a fleeting moment the idea shocked me, but then I started to see how it might not be such a bad thing. He would be caught completely off-guard and I would be able to say my piece and ask him why he had treated David and me so badly.

I was told that he was still in the same neurological ward, and that my agency served that hospital; so with a bit of careful planning I would be able to confront him. I casually asked one nurse, Beth, if she had heard of the doctor; she said yes. I wondered out loud what he was like and she looked at me inquisitively and asked why I wanted to know. I said I knew someone who had been in his care, and quickly asked again what he was like. The response came as no surprise. He was considered aloof and arrogant and had no time at all for the nurses, who he considered far beneath him. She said that people come from all over the country to be treated by him. When I suggested he must be a brilliant doctor she shrugged and said that statistically he was pretty average; his success rate was neither the best nor the worst in the country. I sensed in the way she was talking that Beth was not telling me everything. I can hardly blame her; how did she know how far her words would go? But when I asked her if she would be happy for a member of her family to be treated by Mr Winner, she said "no" without even thinking, and rather emphatically, too. It was a mystery why he was in such demand. I can only imagine that by the time a patient is under his care, it is an emergency so urgent that picking and choosing a neurosurgeon is

150 *Return from Nowhere*

not an option. And it is possible that neurosurgery is such a frontier discipline that a degree of, let's say, experimental failure is expected.

There was another side to the story, too. At this time, the NHS was going through a period of change, with the financial model and the management structure both in a state of flux. I read many a news story about exasperated surgeons, GPs and specialists quitting their jobs or marching over to the private sector in disgust at the way they were being treated by the Department of Health and the managers. Targets were everything, and if this meant a consultation with a child with cancer was limited to three minutes, then so be it. The chances of seeing a GP between 5 p.m. and 9 a.m. or at weekends were slim, partly because this would count as overtime pay (so if you're planning to get ill, try and do it in office hours when it's convenient). Anyone looking from the outside now can see that this is counterproductive, leading to misdiagnoses and missed diagnoses, more serious illnesses and greater expense to the NHS, but those in charge were more concerned with meeting their annual figures before getting their reward of a bonus or a promotion and leaving the issue for someone else to sort out.

I sometimes believe that the NHS is on its way out and the health service is due to return to what it was pre-1945, where healthcare was available but only at a price. Successive governments have seen it go this way, and its demise is happening piece by piece. We only have to look at dentistry; only twenty years ago we were a nation with pretty good dental health because everyone had access to an NHS dentist. Nowadays only a small number of special groups, such as pregnant women and under-18s, qualify for free dental treatment and check-ups. Check-ups are expensive and if treatment is required, it can run into several hundreds of pounds. Dentistry was seen by the decision-makers as non-essential, cosmetic, and there was not a great uproar when it slipped away from the NHS. But dental health is much more than cosmetic, of course. There is gum disease, infection and other oral ailments that are spotted by dentists, not to mention the awful pain of toothache which can make life a living hell, as I well know.

In my work it was impossible to miss the effects of the cuts. I saw badly trained doctors who could barely speak English trying their best but failing to look after patients. There was a training crisis in the country as a whole, which was why so many specialists were, and still are, being drafted in from abroad, often, sadly, from developing countries where they could be of enormous value. It can take the best part of a decade to train up a consultant, and education is of course ongoing as technology is constantly moving on. I met many specialists brought in from abroad and let loose on patients half-trained. The squeeze was also put on us nurses and ancillary staff, with compulsory breaks regularly cancelled, increasing our tiredness and leading to us making mistakes.

* * *

One night, however, during a two-month stint in Victoria General Hospital, I was granted a break, and decided to do something that had been playing on my mind. This was the hospital to which David was admitted after first being assessed correctly at Brookside hospital on his return from abroad. It caused my gut to wrench every time I walked through the main doors. The first few nights in particular had been hard, as I found it difficult to stop my mind constantly rushing back to that time. So this night I resolved to simply go back and look around the actual ward where he had been admitted, partly out of curiosity, and partly, perhaps, to find some closure, although the wound was still wide open.

Wearing my nurse's uniform I could slip from ward to ward without raising eyebrows, even though I was not supposed to stray too far from my allotted area. The neurological ward was easy to find in this large hospital, the route to it imprinted on my mind. The door was locked but a bell was fixed to the wall and without thinking I pushed it. The lock flicked open and I walked through. I was taken aback by how much it had changed. Gone were the corridors and cubicles where I had sat in a daze that first night and with worry on so many other nights. The whole place looked much smaller, too. I do not know how long I had been standing there gazing when a nurse approached me and snapped me out of my trance.

She asked me what I was doing here. I pretended I had come to the wrong place by accident and that I was looking for the MAU, but it was not a very convincing performance – and her face confirmed it. "Well

152   *Return from Nowhere*

you've seen what you wanted to see," she said. "In case you ever get lost again, this ward is 'acute', which it clearly states over the door. And the bell is there for a reason." She softened a little and asked if there was anything she could do to help me. I apologised, shook my head and hurried out of the room, somewhat confused.

When I got back to where I was supposed to be, I asked one of my colleagues where the neurological ward was. She looked puzzled, and asked how long I had been working here, before informing me that there was no longer a neurological ward here – it had been moved to Yale Hospital in Garston, now the clinic of excellence.

There ended my hope of 'bumping into' Mr Winner – for now, at least.

During this time at Victoria General I also had an encounter with a nurse whose face was achingly familiar from somewhere that I just could not put my finger on. She would sometimes catch me staring at her and I thought she must have considered me odd, so one time I took a moment from our busy night to ask her a few questions. It turned out that Mandy had been one of the nurses under Mr Winner when David had been admitted. I remember her being pleasant and down-to-earth, and she still was. We got talking about the doctor and she echoed what Beth had said about him not being liked because of his supercilious ways. And it seemed that his wife had felt the same, as she had left him. Apparently he returned home earlier than expected one day to find her packing her suitcases to leave. Strangely, I actually felt a little bit sorry for him. And I did wonder if the state of his marriage had been affecting his work and his demeanour. My bout of sympathy did not last long, though.

The next day I asked my agency if they could fit me in at Yale Hospital as I was interested in the work there. It was several weeks later when I got the call, at 10 p.m., just as I was relaxing after a lovely bath and thinking about having an early night. This was the way the agencies worked; I was expected to be there as soon as possible as they had apparently been badly let down. I was annoyed at first – after all, I had been awake all day and the prospect of not getting to bed till the next morning made me yawn. I wavered for a moment until the person from the agency reminded me that I had specifically requested work at

Yale, so I was left with little choice but to agree. Would Mr Winner be there, I wondered.

I was told to report to orthopaedics, and when I got there I was greeted by a barrage of chaos, with people going around in all directions. I found out that they were moving everything to another part of the building first thing the following morning and things were being sorted out in preparation. The upheaval was made worse by the fact that this was all happening during the January crisis that was all over the news at this time. A variety of converging events had led to a severe shortage of beds, and hospitals all over the country were admitting only life-threatening emergencies. In my particular hospital a man had just arrived with severe injuries after falling off a ladder. The consultant told me that he had already been turned away from another hospital. With possible head injuries he should not have been travelling in an ambulance any more than necessary.

I asked why he could not be sent to the neurological ward rather than orthopaedics. Daniel the consultant angrily said that those 'sons of bitches' had already turned him away despite his obvious need. He described them as a law unto themselves whom nobody dared challenge. The man was sent to another City hospital. I heard nothing more about him until a few days later when I noticed the headline 'Hospitals turned away coma victim' on 28 January. I read the story and found to my relief that despite the coma, this 39-year-old father of three had survived. According to the story the first hospital to turn him away, Brookside, did not consider his condition to be life-threatening. This all sounded depressingly familiar to me. And Yale Hospital, let us remember, is supposedly a 'neurological centre of excellence'.

Later, Daniel the orthopaedic consultant reiterated his disdain for his neurological counterparts. He told me that not only did they talk down to nurses, but they talked down to the orthopaedic specialists too. Occasionally there would be cause for representatives of several departments to go out to some conference or social event, but the neurologists would form their own clique and ignore everyone else, he said, while those from other disciplines mixed and got to know each other. It's a strange, insular attitude to adopt, especially when medicine of a particular kind often benefits from the advances made in other disciplines.

In the early hours of the morning I was asked to go and find some cot sides in another ward by my supervisor, Marie. As I was leaving she stopped me and said, "Anywhere but the neurological ward. Don't go in there." Feeling that this was a strange request, I nevertheless had not yet found out where the neurological ward was. Not thinking too much about it, I went straight down the corridor and into the next ward. Readers will probably guess which ward I unwittingly plumped for ...

The door was open so I walked in and stood next to the station for a few seconds waiting for someone to see me. I had never in my life experienced such a quiet ward; there was not a soul to be seen or heard. I poked my head around the corner, took a few tentative steps and started saying hello quietly. I noticed there were empty beds, which was strange during such a crisis. I noticed that one of the beds had its curtains drawn around it so I gingerly stepped towards it and whispered hello. There was not a sound. I opened the curtains enough to walk in and was confronted by a bed completely surrounded by silent people who were staring at what I could only imagine was a patient.

The only one to notice me was a blue-clad sister, whose face immediately reddened as she broke from the group and virtually pushed me through the curtains before marching me to the door, scolding me and asking what I was doing there. My explanation did not satisfy her at all; she made sure I was in the corridor and pointed down it to tell me to go away. "Don't come back," she said. I won't, I thought. As I took my first steps away I heard the sister admonishing the nurse who should have been on the station for leaving the door open and abandoning her post.

I finally found some cot sides and returned with them to the orthopaedics. Marie asked why I had been such a long time, albeit in a friendly way. When I told her I went next door first she gasped and said, "That's the neurological ward! I told you not to go there." She forgave me as I was new, but sought my assurance that it would not happen again.

It was only then that I realised that one of the people huddled around the bed could have been Mr Winner. I shuddered, and then asked one of the nurses, Maria, if she knew anyone on the ward. She said not personally, but that her friend had once had a spell there and hated it. When the consultants entered the room nobody was allowed to speak unless spoken to, which in itself was a rare thing. Everyone must remain in absolute silence until they left. It would appear that I had stumbled into their midst during one of these royal visits. And such behaviour would certainly not have been out of character for my particular consultant.

What happened next shocked me; I got a flashback to my fantasies of meting out vengeance on Mr Winner. Only this time it was behind those curtains. What was shocking was that I thought that I had put such images behind me. Intellectually I was sure I would never do anything, of course. I reassured myself that had I wanted him dead, I would not have waited until I was sent to work with him before pouncing. And right now I would no doubt be behind bars. Soon enough, luckily, the rage in me had faded away.

I started to wonder why only the neurological ward had a bell to gain entry. All sorts of ideas crossed my mind, from violence against staff to reprisals from disgruntled mothers. I wondered if it was to protect patients' dignity or maintain doctors' secrecy in their methods. But while these explanations were all conceivably true, they did not explain why none of the other wards had bell entry. I took the opportunity while making the consultant a cup of coffee to put my theories to him. He heard me out and then laughed gently. "No," he said. "The reason it is behind locked doors is because the centre of excellence is funded by private patients, and they need their dignity more than NHS ones do. And it also means that the neurosurgeons have complete and absolute control over who does and does not go in, including which patients they accept. In a way they are autonomous." None of this really surprised me, although I do not know why this explanation had never occurred to me.

I imagine the neurological ward also had the pick of the nursing staff too. Anything that would boost their success rate by a percentage or two would be grasped at; it would all mean more funding and more kudos.

I had had enough experience of nursing staff to know that while many are hardworking, upstanding and conscientious people, there are plenty of them whom I would not trust to look after a goldfish, let alone a sick person. Drug-taking was rife among my fellow workers, both NHS and agency. A coffee or two to get me through the night was my limit, but I was stunned by the number I dealt with who were heavy drinkers or who were taking cannabis, speed or other drugs; Prozac was also a particular favourite. I was shocked as many of these people would no doubt have come face to face with the short- and long-term consequences of drug-taking. They would probably have been sacked had they been caught taking it on the premises but they were so open about it that there must have been a degree of collusive tolerance. Colleagues whom I barely knew would casually tell me what helped them through their shifts. When a male nurse asked me what I was on, I naively thought he was asking me about my wages until he told me he was on cannabis. However irresponsible this attitude, I understand the work is hard, tiring and emotionally draining, and your sleep pattern is constantly being challenged. I think the problem of drink and drug-taking health workers could be greatly reduced simply by improving working conditions, but there is little sign of that happening.

The nurses' treatment of mental health patients also used to annoy me. They seemed able to cope well with horrific accidents, but they dreaded their stints with psychiatric or geriatric patients on their wards, which were becoming more frequent. I think this was because these patients demand more time, both in terms of the daily tasks that need to be performed by the nurse and the fact that often progress is so slow as to be unnoticeable. It hurt me to think that many of the nurses who had dealt with David must have thought of him as someone they would rather not have had to deal with.

The apparently irrational behaviour of some psychiatric patients could cause staff to behave terribly. On one occasion two elderly women with dementia were on the ward, and one of them kept shouting out to Beverley, the nurse on duty. Trying to get some paperwork done Beverley reluctantly stood up to go and attend to the woman, then saw me and asked me to see what she wanted, muttering that they should not even be in this ward and that they were bed-blocking. When I arrived at the bed I pulled the sheets back to find the bed underneath was soaking wet. The elderly woman was incontinent and was lying in a pool of her own urine. I have no idea how long she had been in this inhuman state. It is awful to think that this woman, who had probably lived out her life in dignity and could well have a family who assumed she was being given the best possible care, had been reduced to this, all because a nurse saw only a woman with dementia who was getting in her way.

I was able to accompany the woman to the toilet, and change her bedding and her night-dress. It took a little time, of course, because she was quite frail and unsteady on her feet. But isn't this exactly the type of care nursing staff are supposed to perform, not looking to discharge patients with the minimum of cost? I wonder what Nye Bevan, founder of the NHS, would make of it all.

* * *

Over the coming years I started amassing a collection of newspaper cuttings, notes on television news stories and reports found on the internet on cases of clinical negligence, with a particular emphasis on botched early diagnoses, particularly relating to head injuries. To include all cases of negligence I would have had to hire an assistant, such was the number of the incidents.

It seemed that there was at least one fatal case every week, although the stories were rarely headlines; they were typically tucked away as 'other news' and hard to spot. And usually the story concerned a court case months or years after the event itself. This was like the classic example of road deaths versus plane crashes. If 3,000 people die on the roads in a year, that is about eight every day, or a Boeing 767 full of passengers about every month. A passenger jet crashing every month would not only make global headlines; it would call into question the very concept of passenger air travel. But car crashes might make a ripple in the local newspaper, or perhaps get a mention on the regional news if there are several deaths, but overall, the people do not find out about the number of road deaths until annual statistics come out.

Of course, the national news would need a 20-minute slot to cover all of a day's road accidents. But the way our news is reported can take

158 *Return from Nowhere*

the spotlight off the drip-drip events and thus give a false impression. Fortunately there are not twelve air crashes a week, and air travel is rightly considered among the safest modes of transport there is. But the public uproar that would meet a hypothetical monthly plane crash does not happen with road travel despite the figures being the same.

And so it is with medical negligence. If I were to spread out all my cuttings they would take up the floor of my living room. There is my plane crash. And what is more, it becomes obvious from reading the stories that lessons are not being learnt, because exactly the same things are happening time and time again. The story about people being turned away from a hospital and going on to die is repeated. So are the stories of people failing to have brain scans on MRI or CT scanners because they have their accident outside office hours. We have the technology to peer inside the brain of head accident victims and identify exact locations of lesions and act quickly to stem bleeding or remove objects, but only in office hours. People have done the London Marathon, jumped out of planes and bathed in beans to raise money for their local hospitals to buy these amazing machines. They are not being treated as essential diagnostic tools; in reality, there is usually a waiting list of several months to have a session which takes less than half an hour. Another recurring story is of people being sent home with a box of paracetamol after complaining to A&E of a serious headache, then going on to die of blood clots.

And when I gaze at the plane crash in my folder, I wonder how many *unreported* cases there were, the near misses, the misdiagnoses that were never discovered, the people treated as hopeless cases and never given a chance, the victims persuaded by the hospital that they probably should not bother pursuing their cases through the courts, the elderly head injury victims who simply 'died of old age', and the cases that went to court but were not considered newsworthy, perhaps because they happened on the same day as some celebrity scandal. I am sure my collection is just scraping the surface.

There is another side of the coin, of course, which cannot be ignored. Sometimes deaths and serious deteriorations *are* beyond current medical assistance, and there are plenty of cases where no reasonable person would blame the medical establishment for it. And some people regain their health despite the actions of medical intervention. I fully accept that we are often on the frontiers of science when it comes to treatment of patients.

But not all medical intervention is pioneering. Over time, planned procedures and emergency care become routine as the knowledge gained by early pioneers increases and educates the following generations of specialists. And this is where medical negligence hinders realistic prospects of successful treatment.

I lost count of the number of times I requested that David should have further tests when Mr Winner had said he was satisfactory but when anyone else seeing my son could have said he was not. He probably had such little hope of David surviving that he deemed him not worthy of treatment. But I believe he was negligent and that the technological resources were available to give David the best possible chance of a positive outcome, but that he made a conscious decision not to take advantage of them. Mr Winner's assessment would later find its way to the Department of Social Security, whose three-minute test, alongside the 'professional medical opinion', deemed David fit enough to work and drive a car. I knew he needed constant care and his motor skills were severely weakened so I didn't let him drive until he had improved, but if I had, he could have killed or injured someone. Would the buck have stopped at my door, had that happened? Or the DVLA's? The DSS's? Or Mr Winner's himself? I imagine that my words weighed against such an esteemed member of the medical community would probably not count for much.

There was also the constant threat that what little help David was getting could be cut off completely by the very powers that granted it should I go to the media or kick up a fuss with MPs. It was as though the whole system put a line of defence between David and the financial and medical assistance he was entitled to, and that we should be grateful for any subsistence payments we received.

* * *

Here is one interesting letter I found in *The Times*, under the heading 'A Street Death':

Sir, I am induced to trouble you with this letter, hoping that its insert in your influential columns may induce the police authorities to take every care for the preservation of human life in certain cases requiring immediate medical aid. On the night of the 3rd soon after 10, a gentleman was found by the police near Bow-street station motionless and insensible, removed to the station on a stretcher, charged as drunk, placed in a cell, and soon after 4 next morning found to be dead or dying. Not till then was the police surgeon sent for, who pronounced him dead. A post mortem examination discovered an indication of apoplexy, with an extensive fracture of the skull, and at the inquest a verdict of Death from apoplexy and fracture of the skull from a fall was returned. Two respectable witnesses, in his company a few minutes before he was found, deposed to his perfect sobriety. Surely such facts testify to the inconsiderateness and neglect of the police, who assumed it to be nothing more than a case of drunkenness. A sufferer is found motionless and insensible, and can give no account of himself, the police surgeon lives close by, whose function I presume is to examine immediately all critical cases, and yet the police neglect occasionally to send for him, who can alone judge of their nature, and assume this most grave responsibility to themselves. Even in cases of insensibility from drunkenness which this was not, I know not why the surgeon should not be sent for. It may seem late in addressing you but success has not been had in getting notice taken of the case by those having the control of the police. I feel I shall not have dis-charged my duty without addressing so powerful an agent, and I trust I shall not have applied in vain.

I remain your obedient servant,

H.E.

This letter was from 1862, but its message resonates down the years. With a little linguistic modernisation it could easily pass for an account of an event that took place last week, or certainly in recent years, such has been the lack of real action in such cases.

I saw with my own eyes two cases of people brought into the hospital by police and given short shrift by the medics. Eager to move on to the next patient, they would get frustrated with these slouching, unresponsive patients, and tell them to go somewhere and sober up (despite there being no olfactory or other evidence of their being under the influence of alcohol). The second case in particular was quite heartbreaking, as the same man was brought in several days apart, the second time unshaven and wearing exactly the same clothes and with the same symptoms. Police had found him lying in the street on both occasions. And yet the default diagnosis was drunkenness. This could not be any closer to the bone for me, as David's misdiagnosis in the hours after his accident probably cost him, and by extension his brother and me, several years of our lives as we went through our personal hells.

I read of a story in the *Daily Mail* of a woman who repeatedly, over a period of several months, visited her Burton GP complaining of severe headaches. Migraine was the supposed cause – she was continually told not to worry and sent home without any serious tests. Soon the headaches were affecting her eyesight and stopping her from driving. She went on holiday to France and collapsed soon after her arrival. It was only after she had been rushed to hospital and given a scan that a cancerous tumour was found. It had grown so large that is was making her head swell. When the story went to press, she had been given twelve months to live and was fighting the cancer.

If there is one thing these stories prove it is that the public, the police and most shockingly the health professionals of this country are simply not equipped to deal with head injuries and conditions of the brain. It is hard to ignore the fact that so many life-threatening conditions are being overlooked as drunkenness, migraines or just plain headaches. And that despite the availability of brain scanning devices that are constantly improving in terms of resolution, accuracy, speed and availability, far too many victims are not being given the chance to simply be checked out.

How many false alarms justify not looking for a tumour or haemorrhage? Specialists, GPs, and probably NHS accountants seem to use brain scanning devices as a last resort after a series of questionnaires, thermometers, blood pressure tests and a nice lie down.

Even in the days before CT, MRI, PET, EEG, MEG and NIRS scans, treatment was available and ignored because so few people recognise the symptoms of brain injury. The fact that both it and alcohol abuse can result in stumbling, slurred speech, violence, vomiting and drowsiness, and the fact that sufferers of both can often present with visible head injuries, is unfortunate and has probably led to the death or deterioration of thousands of people over the years. And even if someone is drunk, it does not mean that they have not *also* had a head injury. How a victim is treated depends largely on who finds them and what time of day it is. From the good Samaritan in the street to the neurologist in a high-tech hospital, the initial assumption of drunkenness is hard to overcome at the best of times, but should the victim be found on a Friday night when the hospitals' stomach pumps are going full pelt, or should they unfortunately be a Brit on holiday abroad, you need to be especially diligent to spot the ones who have a brain injury. I realise that if every slurring patient on a Friday night was given a scan, it would probably bring the NHS to its knees, but there has to be a diagnostic procedure that can sort out the plain drunk, the brain damaged and the ones who are drunk *and* brain damaged.

* * *

Alcohol and illegal drugs were never far from my life when I was nursing. As well as the nurses themselves being on all sorts of drugs, I was frequently confronted with the long-term effects of substance abuse. If you ever see a man dying of alcohol-induced liver failure you will never forget it. I still think about a naked man I saw, yellow from head to toe, every time I see a news story about the binge drinking that blights our younger generations, from council estates to university campuses and nightclubs. I remember commenting to my colleague that this patient looked so young, probably in his early thirties, and she confirmed that he was, before adding that he was by no means the youngest victim they had had to look after over the years. This poor man had not been drinking for kicks with his friends. He had nursed his own mother right up to her death, but it had cost him dearly, with his relationship ending and with him turning first to the bottle and then to pure meths in what one can only assume was a mission of self-destruction, to be tragically accomplished any time now.

Not all drug abusers die of their problem, of course, but the sheer number of them is responsible for a hidden problem of mental health and brain damage which is barely noticed by society. If someone is in a road accident, a head injury will probably receive attention if all goes as it should. But there are so many out there who might not even know they have a problem until it is too late, and a lifetime of drug use is a fast-track to such problems. Only after working in a hospital did I really find out the true scale of drug issues in this country.

* * *

My time in hospitals was eye-opening, heartbreaking, heartwarming, and occasionally side-splittingly funny, never knowing what the next five minutes were going to bring. One minute I was nursing someone with minutes to live, the next I was cutting a tangled nightie off an elderly woman with a kitchen knife – to the mirth of everyone on the ward including the entangled woman herself.

I once saw a woman whose leg was covered in maggots, and after my initial disgust, found out that they had been put there on purpose to eat necrotic tissue and stop infection. Modern maggot therapy uses disinfected maggots and can be a very effective way of keeping an open wound clean and safe. It was impossible not to get to know some of the patients personally, and it could be heartbreaking when they died, although we were largely expected to cope with it. People would confide in us, telling us things even their own families might not have known, and although we were usually rushed off our feet, it was inevitable that much of the time we were working with the patients we would also be chatting.

One thing I noticed quite frequently was patients would not just be ill, deteriorate and die. They would be on the road to recovery, make giant leaps from incredibly low points of health and then suddenly die overnight. It was as though they expended all their effort to make progress and then got terminally exhausted in a matter of hours. And while it was sad for us nurses to deal with such occurrences, it was unbelievably hard for the families, who started to build up their hopes and make plans for the future on the strength of their loved one's recovery, only for them to be snatched away before they had the chance to say their goodbyes.

I witnessed mismanagement, or at least the evidence of it, practically every day. There were some wards where understaffing was so severe that I would literally get breathless as I darted from bed to bed. And there were others with eight sleeping patients cared for by two or three nurses, where I would have so little to do that I would get bored. Hospital management is an easy target for newspapers and opposition MPs because managers are seen as overpaid and overprivileged; this is largely true. Although managers and administrators are necessary for the efficient running of such a massive operation, most of those working at the coal face wonder exactly what they are paid for. If a ward got a sudden makeover, with extra cleaning, flowers on the tables and pictures on the walls, you could almost guarantee that it was in preparation for a visit by the health minister. In fact you could probably predict the route the minister would be taking from the car park by the trail of sparkling freshness the cleaning staff would be told to create. The minister would visit and have his photo taken, and then leave confident that the hospital was being well run. But while all this was going on, there would be a ward upstairs where elderly patients snuggled up in their blankets with their teeth chattering thanks to the heating being out of order.

One of the hospitals made national news when it emerged that dead bodies had been piled up in a hospital chapel when they ran out of space in the mortuary, mainly due to a particularly bad flu outbreak. Relatives had turned up and found their loved ones in a heap with complete strangers, each one identifiable by a tag on the big toe. The following day one of my colleagues had to go into the mortuary and was visibly shocked by what she saw, so we can only imagine how painful it must have been for the relatives. Even in a war zone or during a famine, where there is no time to treat bodies with dignity, people try to at least make an effort.

One male patient whom I had got to know a little seemed resigned to his fate as he was terminally ill, but spoke of his happy life and had no regrets. All he seemed to want was a peaceful end. He was quietly inspirational. I popped my head into his cubicle and said goodnight to him as I left to go home at the end of my shift. The following day as I went to say hello to him, I noticed his young grandchild was about to enter; I stopped him and said I would just need to get him ready. At first the man looked like he was asleep, but looking closer, I found that he had died. The staff nurse said she knew that he had died several hours ago, but that they were so short-staffed that there was nobody to move him to the mortuary. So there he had lain in his cubicle, at peace with himself and unaware of the undignified way in which he had been treated; and worse, moments away from being found dead by his family, the first of whom would have been his excited grandson.

It is hard to imagine that man being left there had the health minister been en route: "And if you look to your left, Mr Milburn, you'll see one of our more deceased patients. He'll be moved on when we get a moment."

It is impossible to list all the errors and incompetence I experienced during my time working in the hospitals. I noted most of the stories in my diary and just mention a few here. Those omitted just underline the arrogance, governmental interference, misuse of funds, unprofessionalism, and make-do attitude that exist in the NHS and result in people being drafted in at a moment's notice, often with minimal training or poor grasp of English.

The NHS is so integral to the psyche of the UK that stories of it going wrong often make the headlines and cause much anxiety. But is it any better or worse than the rest of the public or private sector when it comes to competence and trustworthiness? Good news stories rarely make it to the news, but every time there's an MRSA outbreak, a Harold Shipman incident or any other such national story, confidence is chipped away and people start worrying. Many people simply do not bother visiting their GP because they do not trust them or because they have been treated poorly in the past. Apart from the obvious public health implications of such attitudes, this shows how hard the health service has to work just to prevent a catastrophic erosion in public trust.

* * *

I was lucky to be working for an agency at this time, because there was always work available. However, nurses could almost choose the shifts and the hospitals they worked at, and some nurses used somewhat underhand tactics to get more money. For example they would say no if the agency called at relatively short notice, knowing that they might be offered double or triple time to tempt them in to work. The agencies themselves must have been making a fortune. This all came out of the NHS budget, and a Freedom of Information request put the cost of hiring agency nurses at over a billion pounds per year in the mid-2000s. While this was partly down to governmental promises on healthcare, it was also the result of a lack of forward planning by the administrators. Rules about the minimum number of staff on particular wards led to localised overstaffing, but the lack of available staff would also lead to understaffing in other places. And should a hospital attract a few bad stories in the press, the managers would call for all hands on deck and the building would be swarming with staff in no time, half of whom were not sure what they were supposed to be doing.

* * *

Hospital work is certainly not for the faint-hearted, but it is impossible to work in hospitals and not come out with a renewed sense of gratitude and respect for the people who staff them. I have focused on some of the mishaps and misadventures that occurred in my own experience of hospital work, and every nurse will have a similar set of stories to tell. When hospitals are well managed and when nursing staff are not put under so much pressure that they cannot do their jobs properly, hospitals can be inspirational and incredible places. As I like to be kept busy, I found the whole experience stimulating enough to make the terrible moments bearable.

But I can no longer put my trust in the management of hospitals, the governmental departments responsible for making policy or the specialists on whose judgement many of our lives will one day depend. Just a few ranks up the management scale you will be confronted with fear, arrogance and incompetence at critical levels. You will see people covering each other's backs and you will see an endless stream of initiatives coming down from on high, many of which barely have time to be implemented before they are changed. While money being spent on the NHS is never usually seen as a bad thing, the hundred billion pound budget for this enormous behemoth and its million and a half employees (it is the largest employer in the UK) makes it the perfect environment for people to fritter away money with impunity on wasteful projects and policies.

If the same money were better spent, lives would be saved and enhanced. Simple steps such as 24-hour availability of brain scans, which might cost money to implement but would save money in treating the long-term brain damaged, would be logical and sensible. But unfortunately it is not in most governments' or administrators' interests to indulge themselves in long-term thinking. After all, by the time the money is saved they will have left their current posts and will be serving on some corporate board for a few days a year and collecting a six-figure payslip.

The NHS will never be perfect. Healthcare will never be perfect. And my exposure to its inner workings drives home the fact that whatever policies it works under, it will still have to rely on humans to do the work. And since we all make mistakes, there will always be mistakes. But injecting a little accountability, humility and common sense into the whole thing surely would not do it any harm.

I feel I should also challenge the commonly held position that private healthcare is a bed of roses. As an agency worker I have found good and bad in both the public and private health sectors. In some ways the fact that private healthcare is just as flawed is more shocking, as people, whether rich or poor, pay to receive healthcare denied to them on the NHS. Sometimes private health is paid for through insurance payouts after accidents. People forego holidays and home comforts to pay for healthcare. Still, the spotlight rarely falls on private companies.

* * *

My experiences urged me to look at the Hippocratic Oath, the basis of the ethical practice of medicine. It was named after Hippocrates, an ancient Greek physician, who many consider to be the father of medicine as we see it today. Clearly the ancient Greeks did not have the technology available to them that we do now, but they did go about medicine in a

168   *Return from Nowhere*

scientific way, studying anatomy and disease and passing on knowledge to the next generation so that one person's suffering might end up being the basis for another person's relief. The original was in Greek, and starts with a vow to the deities Apollo, Asclepius, Hygieia and Panacea, so it has had to change to move with the times and has been translated into many languages. Nevertheless the thrust of the oath remains more or less intact after several reappraisals. Here is one modern version:

I swear to fulfill, to the best of my ability and judgment, this covenant:

I will respect the hard-won scientific gains of those physicians in whose steps I walk, and gladly share such knowledge as is mine with those who are to follow.

I will apply, for the benefit of the sick, all measures that are required, avoiding those twin traps of overtreatment and therapeutic nihilism.

I will remember that there is art to medicine as well as science, and that warmth, sympathy, and understanding may outweigh the surgeon's knife or the chemist's drug.

I will not be ashamed to say "I know not", nor will I fail to call in my colleagues when the skills of another are needed for a patient's recovery.

I will respect the privacy of my patients, for their problems are not disclosed to me that the world may know. Most especially must I tread with care in matters of life and death. If it is given to me to save a life, all thanks. But it may also be within my power to take a life; this awesome responsibility must be faced with great humbleness and awareness of my own frailty. Above all, I must not play at God.

I will remember that I do not treat a fever chart, a cancerous growth, but a sick human being, whose illness may affect the person's family and economic stability. My responsibility includes these related problems, if I am to care adequately for the sick.

I will prevent disease whenever I can, for prevention is preferable to cure.

I will remember that I remain a member of society with special obligations to all my fellow human beings, those sound of mind and body as well as the infirm.

If I do not violate this oath, may I enjoy life and art, respected while I live and remembered with affection thereafter. May I always act so as to preserve the finest traditions of my calling and may I long experience the joy of healing those who seek my help.

Source: Wikipedia, 29 October 2011

Fine words indeed, notable for their humility, compassion and thirst for progress. If only they were obeyed. If only they could be made to apply to institutions and government departments as well as individuals.

There is no mention in the oath of leaving patients lying in their own urine because of a shortage of sheets. Nothing on turning away sick patients because hospitals are full. Nothing about rushing nursing staff off their feet. Nothing about talking down to those tasked with assisting you. Nothing about covering up botched operations or passing the blame (in fact it is notable in taking the opposite stance – 'I will not be ashamed to say "I know not"' – admitting your mistakes and learning from them to prevent the same mistakes from being repeated).

I wonder how often people working in the health services ever look at this fundamental oath to remind themselves of the intensely important job the rest of the nation are entrusting them with.

11

Against my better judgement

With December looming, my mind had started to become occupied by the court case that I hoped would bring this whole nightmare to some sort of conclusion. Although I knew that no arrangement would make our lives suddenly become easy, at least we could achieve some sort of stability and start to make plans for the future.

I still had huge financial problems, and was managing by scrimping and borrowing, but this could not go on indefinitely. My financial needs were way above those of the average mother and their impact was demoralising for the whole family. As the days passed and the court date got closer, my emotions oscillated between fear and foreboding, and optimism. Until the court case, there was nothing but routine, fatigue and helplessness, as unlike when David was at BIF, I had no chance to rest or time to myself. Then a letter came through the door. Case deferred. No new date. I was devastated and this time my anorexia started in earnest.

I asked Elaine, my solicitor, why the case had been deferred. She said that initially the medical defence had not taken the case seriously but then something had given them a wake-up call so they had requested the deferral so they could put a case together. This seemed totally unfair to me, but I was powerless to take any action. At first they had tried to fob us off saying that they had no case to answer. When that had failed, they had tried to claim that the three-year time limit had passed, knowing full well that the clock did not start ticking until negligence had been *discovered*, not from when it had been perpetrated. So because their attempts to scupper my claim had failed and this hearing really was going ahead, they were granted extra time to prepare a case. I am sure no extra time would have been given to me had the roles been reversed.

Still, Elaine encouraged me by pointing out that even though it all seemed unjust, the courts would not tolerate any silly games, and must have been given a very convincing reason to postpone – they would nevertheless want the case settled as soon as possible.

In the meantime, she went before a medical defences committee to try and get the postponement lifted. To our joy she succeeded. The judge was dismissive of the behaviour of the medical defence's legal team, and informed them that they had had enough time to present a case. This got the wheels of justice moving in a way we hadn't expected. Not long afterwards my phone rang and Elaine, sounding upbeat, said, "I've got an early Christmas present for you." I assumed it would be a date for the court case. "They have admitted liability! They have admitted that Mr Winner caused David's brain damage!"

I gasped. For a few moments I did not know what to say. I tried to thank Elaine, but the words just came out as a rattled set of syllables. Regaining my composure, I became first elated and then disgusted by the tactics of the medical defence. Clearly they had known they were guilty all along but had assumed I would believe their side of the story and be either intimidated or demoralised by their delaying tricks. I will never know how close they were to succeeding and I was shocked beyond belief.

This turn of events felt like a fog clearing from my mind, but it was effectively meaningless until the admission of guilt resulted in some kind of action. My primary concern was that David should receive recompense, ideally back-paid, for the negligence and the financial and emotional distress he had suffered. If Mr Winner could be disciplined, retrained or struck off – made to face up to the reality of the situation – that would be great. And finally if wider lessons could be learnt not only about emergency brain treatment but also about the care of those affected by brain damage, I would at least feel some sense of closure.

The date for the hearing finally came six months after the original date. Surely this time it would go ahead.

And of course, the medical defence team regrouped and started scheming again. They changed their admission from liability to partial liability, citing the abrupt cessation of David's medication as the cause of his deteriorating condition thereafter. They claimed that even after his first haemorrhage, he might have been epileptic for life as the epilepsy had been caused by the haemorrhage itself. But this was simply not true. Over a couple of years, his epilepsy had got steadily worse, entirely due to his medication being erroneously withdrawn by the hospital. I expressed my shock to Elaine at the audacity of these people, and started to feel myself sinking again. But she reassured me that even limited liability is still serious and points the finger at them. They would not be able to wriggle free indefinitely.

Three months before the rearranged date of the hearing I had a meeting with the clinical negligence specialist barrister, Richard Mortimer QC, in Preston to assess the cost of care so I could make my claim. The rehabilitation specialist and the psychologist were also in attendance as well as Elaine, David, John and I. At the start I got the impression that the QC did not fully understand the case, but as the day went on and after much emotional pleading and explanation of the situation, he seemed to grasp it. At the conclusion of the meeting he agreed with us that David really did need round-the-clock care.

There then followed a painful wait for the final court appearance. I was frightened but optimistic, and maybe even a little excited. I relished the chance to get off my chest more than a decade's worth of pain and ignorance that had had such a chilling result. Perhaps I was naïve, or simply unable to cope with the prospect of losing at this late stage. If the case failed, there would almost certainly be no starting again.

The night before the appearance I made a point of going to bed early so I would be alert to the slightest hint of trickery on the part of the medical defence lawyers. But I couldn't sleep that night. There was a tornado of emotion and little notes and reminders flurrying around my brain.

I probably snatched a few hours' sleep; I certainly remember being woken up by my alarm on that fateful Friday. I faced myself in the mirror and sighed at the ashen look that the years had given me. Trying to look strong and uncowed, I applied a little make-up. My hands were shaking and I was a little out of practice, but I managed to erase some of the visible pain. I was putting my smartest clothes on when the phone rang.

Elaine told me not to worry, but that there would be a slight delay while a technicality was sorted out. Her words might have been intended to be reassuring but I sensed a hesitancy and a flakiness that began to erode the optimism that she had inflated me with and that had got me to this point. What now?

I got into the car with David and was in no fit state to drive. Everything seemed to be crawling along and I had to give every press of the pedals and turn of the steering wheel my utmost attention. I had to pull myself together, and fast.

Luckily, I did reach the courthouse in one piece. We were led into a side room, where I was surprised to see Professor Roberts, the psychologist. He had turned down a place at a conference in Geneva that day to give us his support, and how invaluable that turned out to be (I was incredibly touched when I later found out that he had paid his expenses out of his own pocket). Elaine approached me and again said that there was a technicality that needed sorting out. She was confident that the defence solicitors would be making an offer at the earliest opportunity, but I did not share her optimism. Surely they would have done so by now if they thought they could avoid a potentially costly court appearance and verdict?

We started to walk along the corridor towards the courtroom, my heart pounding, and. I saw Richard Mortimer QC hurrying towards us. He had just had a meeting with their team. He stopped us and gathered us round in a huddle. "They have offered us £1.5 million," he said. "What do you want to do?" Before I could construct an intelligible sentence, we were ushered into the main courtroom and the defence solicitors started to ask the judge, Justice Charles Simpson, for burden of proof.

My team was taken by surprise by this manoeuvring. We knew the offer was not high enough. It had been made at the last possible second, no doubt so I would come to a snap decision. And then within seconds it had effectively been withdrawn. Elaine was not used to this kind of behaviour, and I was disoriented and shocked. In the courtroom there followed several minutes of frenetic activity that I could only observe.

174   *Return from Nowhere*

There was a murmur of impenetrable legalistic talk as Professor Roberts scribbled notes and passed them to my solicitor and my QC. Then all of a sudden proceedings were brought to an end; we were told to stand and the judge walked out of the room. We followed moments later.

Elaine suggested that coffee was in order, and over the steaming cups she explained that the defence team had put a legal technicality before the judge and that he had retired to consider it. We would be called back in no time, she assured me, and it was nothing unusual.

We had barely finished our last drops before we were being whisked back again. The judge had rejected the technicality argument and found in our favour. I looked over at the medical defence team and was buoyed to see for the first time it was their turn to look concerned. I could feel a tidal change coming, but not quite yet. The judge asked our QC if we could settle this without a trial, but Mr Mortimer shook his head and said that an offer had been made which fell far short of our calculated position. Unmoved, the judge reminded us that it was a Friday and that the cost to the public purse of a trial would be considerable. He urged us to do all we could over the weekend to bring this disagreement to an amicable conclusion that obviated the need for a trial. If we could not come to an agreement, he would make the decision himself.

As we filed out of the court, I was still in a daze about what had gone on. Elaine told me that the claim of burden of proof made by the defence was an attempt to shift the onus on to us to prove beyond reasonable doubt that David would have made a full recovery if Mr Winner had not failed in his duties and had instead given David the operation after the first haemorrhage. On the face of it, this would have been extremely difficult to prove as even a slight doubt about the guilt of the accused can result in the collapse of a prosecution. But thanks to the quick thinking of my team, particularly Professor Roberts, the defence's claim was rejected outright by the judge. I realised that eleven years of fighting, and David's future, could have rested on the judge swinging the other way on what was a fiendishly technical point. Indeed, another judge, or even the same judge on a different day, might have sided with the defence.

Our barrister had presented a claim for £3 million, which would cover David from the time since the accident and for the rest of his life, during which he was unlikely ever to work again and would need constant care. As I thought back over the words and tone of the judge, I felt he was not in a mood for games by the defence team and would want the case settled with the defence paying what we had asked for.

The more I thought about the trick the defence team had tried to pull, the angrier I got. The sum of £1.5 million might not sound like a pittance to most people, but would not cover all David's potential costs. If David went on to have a normal lifespan, he would need money for sixty years or more of housing, care, clothing and food. Someone on an average salary of £33,000 would earn that much in just forty-five years and so would need more for another fifteen years. Also, David's living costs were much higher than average due to his need for care. I knew that a weekend of worry lay ahead of me. If no agreement was made, would that look bad for us or for the defence? I could not ignore the risk that I was taking by pursuing this cause. If David were to lose his case, and effectively be deemed fit and well, I might end up having to pay a large contribution towards not only the court costs but also the care he had received thus far, which already ran into a few hundred thousand pounds. It would be impossible for me to pay all of it, and I would no doubt have to sell my home.

I began to shake all over again, and worried about driving home safely. But it was important that David did not sense my inner turmoil. He needed me to be strong, and I tried my best. Somehow I did manage to make it home, where I went straight to bed and to sleep, leaving David alone in the living room.

The next morning I awoke with a start and rushed into the living room, expecting to find my son cold and hungry. But he had made his way to bed too, I was relieved to discover.

As the weekend progressed my emotional state hardly calmed down. Again I felt peaks and troughs of fear, anger, apprehension and, occasionally, optimism. But all it took was a glimpse of David's face and I would involuntarily smile. That was who all this was for, and whatever they threw at me, he would still be there. He had a sort of childlike innocence about him, which was both worrying and also comforting, as he probably grasped only a little of what was happening on his behalf.

Monday came and early in the morning Elaine was on the phone. She told me the defence team had made an offer of £1.5 million – no higher than that offered three days earlier. I wondered what they were playing at. Why would I reject an offer on Friday only to accept it on Monday, particularly as the wind seemed to be in our sails, not theirs? Perhaps they hadn't expected their offer on Friday to be accepted immediately, as I didn't get the chance to accept or reject it formally. Perhaps they thought a weekend of worry about the cost of losing would have softened up my resolve. They could afford to play these games, of course. It would not be their money that would be lost; indeed they were no doubt charging some exorbitant hourly rate.

Ironically, had I known about their burden of proof claim before they made their offer, I might well have taken it just to cut our potential losses. But I was not about to give in now. I did not think the judge would be happy about a weekend of silence followed by exactly the same offer, when we were supposed to be negotiating an arrangement, so I refused.

Several minutes later the phone rang again with £1.75 million. I refused again, but sensing a game of cat and mouse, I gave Elaine my lowest price: £2 million. If they refused, it was up to the judge.

Elaine called their solicitors, and again came back with an offer. They would pay the £2 million, but the costs to date would have to come out of that. I flatly rejected it, feeling a little exasperated with Elaine because she seemed to be saying that their offer was fair. Of course, she was supposed to be able to gauge my chances of success and the size of any award, so perhaps she too was getting nervous about a disadvantageous judgement (and maybe about her own fees being paid, too). But after a whole day spent calculating the past, present and future costs of David's care and coming to a figure of £3 million, why should we pull back now? I was losing faith in my own solicitor, even though I still felt the judge was leaning my way. Plus, I wanted my day in court. I was ready now to spill eleven years' worth of hurt.

But just as I was about to leave for court the phone rang again. They had agreed £2 million with no costs. I reluctantly accepted, but heard we would still have to go to court to formalise the offer.

Against my better judgement

It transpired this was another trick by the defence who denied making the verbal offer. I think they were trying to make me think that they knew something I did not, but I saw their offers as admissions of guilt.

Once at court, it proved to be a last-gasp contrivance to make me accept a smaller award and pay the costs, because with little further action the out of court settlement was agreed, albeit without admission of liability. I was apprehensive about accepting a million pounds less than the calculated cost. But being able to finally draw a line under proceedings and not having to take a gamble with the inscrutable judge balancing our competing claims seemed like the least risky option. I had managed to raise the stakes a little, and I think this surprised the legal team.

Still, the game was over for both legal teams. And it was merely a game, a bit of staged arguing carrying no real weight beyond bragging rights and badges of success should the side they are arbitrarily allocated happen to win. The disappointed looks on their faces quickly faded as they commiserated with each other, as though a game of bar-room pool had been lost, and made arrangements for dinner that night, no doubt at some exclusive restaurant.

* * *

Long before courts had become involved, and when I still had total faith in Elaine, I had asked her if she would deal with any money that came David's way should our claim be successful. Having no experience of dealing with large sums of money, I was anxious to invest wisely for David's future. I also wanted it to be clear that every penny should go directly to help David and, even though I had been impoverished by events, I did not want anyone to think that I might benefit myself in any way. I felt confident that I would be able to get back on my feet again as long as David was cared for.

However, in the event Elaine said albeit would be illegal for her to take power of attorney. I could see that allowing the very solicitor who is fighting the cause to take responsibility for a person's wealth would be open to abuse. She did, however, recommend a colleague called Thomas Hughes, who had already dealt with similar cases, though she warned me it would probably take about three months to do the paperwork, as well as criminal and bankruptcy checks and such like.

In what felt like a wrapping-up conversation, Elaine and I chatted about how far we had come and agreed that the outcome had probably been better than either of us would have dreamt of several years ago. But then she seemed to make out that now these legal affairs were over, I could get on with my life and David would now be someone else's responsibility. I could not believe that she thought I had been through all this to get rid of him. I still wanted to be as big a part of David's life as he wanted me to be. If he wanted independence, now he would be in a better position to achieve it, but as members of a close family we would still look after each other through thick and thin. I found Elaine's comment very hurtful. I had certainly said that looking after David had worn me out, but I didn't want to leave him behind now. The fact that I did not know what to do with £2 million was why I needed help. Elaine's suggestion that someone such as Thomas would not only oversee the financial arrangements but also attempt to meet his unique care requirements was out of the question.

Although in some ways I owed everything to Elaine, towards the end of our dealings together I did wonder if my case, or maybe I, was beginning to grate on her, as she did seem to become a little condescending towards me.

I took my concerns to Thomas who more or less confirmed in legal terms what Elaine had said, namely that an official receiver had overall say on all matters of his or her charges, although my opinions would 'be taken into account' as I was the one most familiar with David and his needs. This did not seem right, so I went away and did a little research.

A few days later I called Thomas's office and his receptionist, having told me he was too busy to speak to me, passed me on to a Kathleen Pearson, who was now, apparently, David's receiver! This really concerned me. Once I had made an appointment to meet her, she asked me to sign a few papers. She often would not speak to me on the phone or return my calls. Then she started asking me to come and see her almost every other day to sign this or that, which became quite a trial. Her answers to my questions about the receivership were at best vague and at worst postponed for eternity. I felt I was being swept along in something I did not understand, and was again powerless, as I had absolutely no idea what to do with the money otherwise. I could not put it in my bank account. Could it go in a trust fund, or an account in David's name? There seemed to be no help available.

I took my concerns to Elaine, who laughed them off, saying I needed a holiday. Most disturbingly, though, she said that if I was short of money she could access the funds already and get a little advance. Then she asked if there was anything else David needed. Hearing that our TV was almost functionless, she worked out a sum of money for a new one and a holiday, and said she would sort out the cash. I did not like the way that she was treating David's money as a lottery win, although she seemed to think that that was what it was.

Eventually I told Elaine that I had no faith in Kathleen and that I no longer wanted her to be in control of my son's finances and, by extension, his life. "She'll be fine," she said. "She's still learning." Was I supposed to heave a sigh of relief at this point? I pointed out to Elaine that on her recommendation I had chosen Thomas, because he was supposedly experienced in such matters. But then, without my knowledge, the responsibility had been passed to someone for whom David would be a guinea pig. I told her that I would have to take responsibility for his money from now on because unfortunately I could not trust her protégé.

Elaine looked me in the eye and said, "Are you sure that's the reason, and not something else?" I shook my head and asked her what she meant by that, but she just turned and walked off.

When I got home I phoned BIF to see if they could offer any advice. They must have dealt with cases like David's in the past. They recommended a company called Thompson Franks, a specialist investor for victims of clinical negligence awards. And they were presumably not learning on the job.

* * *

We did, however, take Elaine's advice on one point at least – a holiday. We went off to Spain for a fortnight, and I think it probably did us all good in the short term, even though I was constantly thinking about what was happening on David's behalf back home. In hindsight, I wish I had put the holiday off.

I called in to see Elaine and the game had changed somewhat. Whenever I requested money for David, I would have to ask her, she would have to claim it and there would be charges involved. I was shocked to find out that the charge was £200 per transaction, literally every time he needed money. Even by solicitors' other-worldly charging standards, this was quite a breathtaking fee. I shuddered to think how quickly the pot would shrink this way. Again, Elaine was acting as though money was no object to me now, as if I was some latter-day Viv Nicholson, the famous pools winner ready to spend, spend, spend. Of course the truth was completely different. I had fought, become anorexic, begged and suffered for eleven years, throughout which my sole purpose was to secure a good life for my son, and now that at least a glimmer of a prospect had been found, I risked giving half of it away to the very solicitor who had a few months earlier urged me to accept a much smaller amount. I reminded Elaine that I had asked for responsibility to be transferred back to me and she said the wheels were in motion but she wanted me to reconsider. I thought it unlikely that she had even started proceedings.

Although I was troubled by the way the solicitors were handling the case, a chat with one of the other experts who had helped David win his case made my mind up. He seemed genuinely alarmed when I told him about the receivership being passed to the solicitors, and asked me why I was not taking it on myself. When I told him about my own lack of confidence in the matter, he went quiet for a moment and then tried to change the subject. Maybe he did not want to offend me by making out that he knew better than me, or maybe he did not want to say anything controversial about the solicitors, but when pressed, he said that I was the one who had David's best interests at heart. Anyone else would be in it for the money.

In the meantime, I was asked by Elaine to attend a few meetings with the QC and a group of three accountants regarding David's investment. I questioned why accountants were present and not, for example, a bank manager, fund manager or other investment experts. In no uncertain terms I was told that this was really not my business and that the ultimate decisions lay with them. (I would later find out that her husband was an accountant, and although I never found concrete proof, I suspected that the accountants could have been from his firm.) More worryingly, I found out that these accountants were being paid £1,000 each for merely attending each meeting. I believe the kind of financial advice they were offering would normally be given for free, perhaps with a commission on any profits made by the vehicles they suggested.

The waters got murkier as I delved deeper. I was seen as something of a goose with a golden egg, particularly to Elaine, who had been made a partner of her firm of solicitors on the back of David's case. I knew that her firm, Parsons and Partners, were paid a few hundred thousand for their work with David's case. I found out that although Elaine advised me she was not profiting personally from any investments on David's behalf and was supposedly arranging these meetings out of the goodness of her heart, if David's money had been invested via these accountants, Parsons and Partners would have stood to get a £60,000 referral fee.

I had almost grown used to being taken advantage of, but the way these people descended on David's money to use it for their own ends practically destroyed my faith in their professions. Most of the people who had let me down – the specialists, consultants, solicitors and accountants – are so esteemed in society that they would be sought as a reference for a passport application. They do not get where they are by being timid, of course, but a degree of humility and honesty is the least you would expect from them. At one point Elaine arranged for an assessor from a private care company to come to my house to weigh up David's needs and ensure he was being properly cared for. Although I was glad of the prospect of help, I had been looking after him for eleven years and knew what he needed. Elaine reminded me that the terms of the settlement did state that David needed 24-hour care, and that that accounted for the size of the payout. Not only had Elaine gone over my head and sorted out a carer without my knowledge, but when I asked her how much they charged, she said, "It's not your money, don't forget – it's David's. And in any case, he has plenty." Once again I felt powerless and overwhelmed by events. When I questioned whether the money was being spent too freely and whether alternative providers had been asked for a quote, Elaine had reminded me that she was legally in charge of his money, and there was no real argument against that.

What Elaine could never have known was that 24-hour care in David's case was not round-the-clock intensive care; it was merely that he could not be completely self-sufficient. I knew that David spent much of the time simply relaxing or asleep, as a result of his haemorrhages. He simply needed more rest than healthy people and there was no point in having a carer by his side all the time, not least because he did not like being crowded or fussed over. To be fair, the private healthcare company saw this too, and decided that the best option would be for any care to be from late morning to early evening.

When I had said I wanted what was best for David, some of those dealing with his finances jumped to the conclusion that I had meant that I would be looking after him (and his money) at my house. In fact, over several discussions, it was concluded that he would be best served by having a degree of independence in his own house, albeit with care, both professional and provided by his family. And that was our ultimate aim.

My relationship with Elaine became even more strained over this transitional period. I was glad I had not signed everything over to her or one of her chosen ones, because I still had some legal power over David's compensation, despite her hints that I did not. Our conversations would be short and businesslike, never friendly or familiar. As her grip on the money got looser, she would resort to ever more underhand tactics to try and persuade me that I was incapable of looking after it.

I made an appointment for a representative of Thompson Franks, the award investment specialists recommended by BIF, to come and visit me to talk over David's case. Coincidentally, on the day that Neil Murray came round, Michael Collins, owner of the private healthcare company, Collins Case Management, was also at my house. I was a little surprised to see that they were on first-name terms, although on reflection it would have been stranger if their paths had never crossed.

I waited until Michael had left before I told Neil the whole story. He seemed to understand everything perfectly. He was quite surprised though at the attitude of the solicitors, and assured me that it was perfectly possible for one party to look after the actual financial investment while another had access to it and cared for the person at the centre. This was in contrast to the beliefs Elaine had put into my mind, namely that I was incapable of looking after David's award.

A few days later I heard that Collins had booked a hotel suite in Manchester, to hold interviews for the position of David's carers. I had no idea why the interviews could not have been held in Collins's perfectly adequate offices. Still, they were probably not paying for it. It was just another example of the way David's money, his future, was being thrown around. I kicked up a fuss about the needless use of a hotel, and in the end the solicitors allegedly paid for it, possibly using David's funds. The gaggle of solicitors, accountants and the barrister continued to try to put obstacles in the way of my taking receivership of David's award. They invited me to one meeting, seemingly to belittle and humiliate me, referring to me in the third person and asking me directly if I planned to buy a Spanish villa with the money or whether I had ever been declared bankrupt.

The next time I attended a meeting I took my old confidante Lucy Bowen from the Brainstorm charity with me. She looked the part, all suited up and businesslike with a briefcase, and took notes throughout the meeting. It knocked barrister Richard Mortimer and his colleagues off their stride. But even with this witness in the room, Richard could not resist a few jabs and body blows. An investment was mooted that more or less tied David to the same house for the rest of his life, albeit with a regular monthly income. When I objected to it, suggesting that one day he might want to get married and buy a new home with his wife, Richard laughed, saying it was unlikely to happen unless David "was to have a brain transplant". I was horrified by the callousness of this remark and even his colleagues sat there open mouthed in surprise.

Throughout the rest of the meeting, I acted the simpleton that he inferred I was, asking them to explain everything several times, to their obvious irritation. Lucy's presence definitely tempered their tendency to belittle me, particularly since she was writing everything down. After an accountant explained something particularly poorly for the second time, he asked in a low hiss if I understood it yet. When I shook my head he almost threw his papers on the ground with rage, muttering "I'm not being paid for this", even though there were bundles of Parsons and Partners papers tied with blue ribbons (the ribbons associated with court papers) all over his desk. "Trust me," he said, "I am a professional. I know what I am talking about." I said I could not agree to something I did not understand, and could not allow my son's award to be invested in a scheme I did not approve of. With Lucy taking notes, I was free to listen to the nuances of their words, and give more considered responses. I think they had been assured that I would be a pushover, and had expected to blind me with complexity and thinly veiled legal threats; however, I realised that no matter what they had led me to believe, they had no legal right to look after what was rightfully David's. When I asked the barrister why this particular care company had been chosen from so many available, he admitted that it was the one providing the care for his own mother. This answered a lot of questions that had been going round in my head. Although he may not have gained anything from this meeting, he must have been benefiting from this recommendation and others in some way. Eventually, when Richard looked at his watch and declared the meeting over, it seemed he had become aware that perhaps this whole affair was over.

As we walked out of the meeting, Elaine invited me back to her office to talk things over.

"What do you want to talk about?" I asked.

"I want you to reconsider taking over the receivership."

"Then we have nothing to discuss," I calmly responded, although I could feel the adrenalin flowing.

Driving home, Lucy and I laughed out loud. We had completely destroyed the little coterie that Elaine had assembled. No doubt they had all been excited about how much money they could make. It certainly would have been enough to grant Elaine a lucrative position in her company and enough to get some rather expensive accountants and a high-ranking barrister involved. We hoped Elaine would have some serious explaining to do to her paymasters and to those she had seduced into the scheme.

Unfortunately, my involvement with Elaine and her company was not over. They still had some control, and, shamefully, from then on, Elaine doubled the £200 transaction fee to £400, and there was nothing I could do about it.

* * *

My next challenge – and disappointment – was dealing with the carers chosen to look after David. One had a background that included work with the WTRC and the other had worked at BIF. Everything seemed fine at the start, but soon they started to realise how they could take advantage of David and had no qualms about doing so. I found out that Simon, who was having relationship problems, would drive David to his girlfriend's house and then leave him outside in the car waiting for hours at a time while he went inside with his girlfriend. Soon Simon also became lazy and unreliable. Jack was not quite as bad, but was forgetful and disrespectful, and wasted a lot of David's time taking him on his personal errands. Both 'carers' knew the size of David's award and treated him like a benevolent millionaire or their best friend, whichever suited them at the time, and raised their voices to him threateningly when he showed defiance. I shudder to think of the ones who failed the interview.

One day when David was in Michael Collins's office he overheard him saying to a colleague, "In this game you can write your own blank cheques." I gave the care company a call and told them that I wanted them to hold fire for now, and that I would be back in touch when I had full receivership.

Soon afterwards I got a letter from the court, asking why large amounts of money were being taken out of David's award all of a sudden. For the short period when just John and I had been caring for him, nothing had gone out, but now the withdrawals were running into the thousands. No wonder they were suspicious. I wrote back straight away saying that the receivership was currently in the hands of the solicitors and that I had no access to it except through them. I let it be known that I was not happy about the situation. I found out that £3,000 had gone to Kathleen Pearson even though she had done absolutely nothing – and even Elaine had admitted she was training. And I worked out that had the care costs carried on as they had been going, the money would have run out in just twelve years.

I wrote to tell Elaine what had happened and instruct her to curb her spending, but characteristically she laughed it off, saying there was plenty of money. Had I not met Neil Murray, who spent hours selflessly explaining everything and advising me, I do not know if I would have been able to extricate myself from the position I was in. He advised me to set up a structured settlement that would ensure David had money for the rest of his life, but not to invest all of it, as there would always be the need to access funds, whereas Elaine had said that it should all be invested, no doubt for suitable remuneration. Over months relations between Elaine and me broke down and she repeatedly fobbed me off when I got in touch with her. Eventually her PA told me that I would have to do all my business through her, supposedly after I had raised my voice and sworn at Elaine, which was absolutely untrue. My own financial situation was beginning to cripple me because I refused on principle to let Elaine have £400 of my son's money every time he needed some. I went deep into my overdraft instead.

On one occasion I managed to get through to Elaine herself. There was still no movement on the change of hands, and she attempted to shoo me away by saying that these things take time and that the courts were busy. Following this conversation, I spoke to Neil again, telling him of my frustration over the delay. He advised me that the delay was down to Elaine who had overstepped her authority by contacting the court of protection, insisting that I was unfit to take over the receivership on David's behalf, and requesting that they grant her office the receivership as previously requested. This unprecedented approach shocked both Neil and me to the core, and drained the last of my confidence in Elaine and her legal team. Plus, she said, they were awaiting the results of some test case that might affect David's award. I had had enough of this time-wasting, so told her that I was going to contact the 'Office for the Supervisor of Solicitors'. She went quiet for a few moments, before mumbling something about having nothing to hide.

Against my better judgement **187**

Remembering something else I'd wanted to say, I called back ten minutes later and was told by Elaine's PA, Mary, that I could not speak to her as Elaine was going through a large pile of files. This brought a smile to my face. Was she panicking? I got a hint that Mary was not too upset about any worries her boss might have had, and it would not have surprised me to learn that she did not have much respect for her either. Mary had also kindly tipped me off during a previous conversation that all my future calls were to be recorded.

Another year had passed and still there was no progress. Eventually the medical defence team started putting pressure on the QC and Elaine to sort out the way David's award was to be invested – they set a time limit for a structured settlement or the option could be lost altogether. Elaine got in touch trying to persuade me to agree to a £750,000 structured settlement rather than the £500,000 (non returnable). After calculating with Neil which option would give David a fixed monthly income for the rest of his life, I wanted to take the £500,000 and leave the remainder with the court, in the hope that when David eventually had more freedom, we could invest the remainder in a way that would give him better access to it. I said, "I refuse to be moved on this." On the day the QC Richard Mortimer went to finalise the settlement, Elaine phoned to ask one last time if I would agree to £750,000. I flatly refused, but hours later, I discovered that they had ignored what I had said and settled for this very amount. I was furious that once again someone had overstepped their authority, and gone against my explicit instructions.

I talked it over with Neil as soon as I heard, and he was just as surprised as I was. But he consoled me by saying that at least this would mean more income for David for the rest of his life, even if the remainder of the settlement ran out. Yet another shock hit me when I discovered that Elaine had misinformed me on the amount of time the settlement would take to finalise, estimating six months because the presiding judge was a circuit judge. I wrote directly to the judge to find out if it could be sped along and was surprised to get a reply just days later. He said that in fact the arrangement had already been agreed, three months previously! I will always wonder if Elaine had tried to buy time so that she could make Kathleen Pearson the official receiver and

188   *Return from Nowhere*

then tell me that it was too late to do anything about it. I called Elaine straight away to find out why she had not let me know and she replied, "Oh, sorry; it must have slipped my mind." A few days later the official notification letter came from Parsons.

All the evidence points to an organisation trying to take full advantage of any awards that David might win. The money, intended to look after David for the rest of his life, was simply too tempting. And during the brief time when it was in her control, Elaine amply demonstrated how she was going to treat it – as a windfall.

I got an opportunity to talk over my case with a court official, who told me that despite all the pain and mental stress the whole affair had caused me, I was actually one of the lucky ones. This sort of thing goes on all the time, and I was lucky to have discovered – quite by chance – that Kathleen was going to be given receivership. Otherwise, our battle would have been much more of an uphill one. Elaine even tried to pull the wool over my eyes about the interest that was due, saying there was none as it simply did not work like that. I checked with Neil and sure enough, there was quite a lot of interest due. I demanded that this was backdated, and she had no choice but to reluctantly agree. She looked at me inquisitively and said, "You must be getting advice from someone. Who is it?" She went on to blame the defence solicitors for the subsequent delays in the delivery of the back-payments, but Neil, who had contacts in the NHS, had assured me that the payment had cleared, so was in the possession of none other than Parsons, earning interest. When the interest was finally paid to David, it came to precisely £21,328.84: no small amount.

How ironic it was that ever since our relationship had soured, Elaine had accused *me* of wanting to get my hands on David's money, jumping on me every time I said "our" instead of "his". In reality she was the one who wanted it, for her own purposes and to pay her connections their exorbitant fees for services that were practically non-existent. I had intended to put in a complaint about the conduct of both Elaine and Richard Mortimer, once I finally got the receivership, but by then I was completely exhausted. Instead I invested my energy in making sure everything was in place for David's future needs, learning as I went along how to be the official receiver.

Against my better judgement **189**

* * *

You might be reading this book because you have suffered, or are suffering, from a situation similar to what my family and I had to go through. You might think that because people in general are caring and conscientious, that the professionals who you entrust with your case will also be looking out for your interests. But as we have seen, this is not necessarily the case. Some people will sense weakness and try to take advantage of you while ostensibly fighting your cause. They will try to blind you with specialist knowledge and brainwash you into trusting them. But what they might forget is that when faced with a dire situation, you too can become an expert in the field. You can work out the path that events should take and become suspicious when events deviate from it. It is incredibly important to recognise that you are suspicious and not paranoid. Suspicion is the defence mechanism that can prevent major abuses taking place, and it is entirely logical.

And it is also important to realise that there are people who are genuine, too. They might not be the touchy-feely ones, who are always reminding you of their religious faith or charitable work. They might be those who quietly go about their work and do it well. There will be people earning money from the very fact that you have suffered a misfortune, from the person changing your hospital bedding to the barrister who represents you. Medics, lawyers and accountants are generally paid pretty well, and most of them deserve it. But there are lines that should not be crossed in the search for remuneration. Unfortunately we must keep on our guard even when we are at our weakest, and not assume that compassion is the default state. Trust has to be earned, never assumed. The good news is that some people will earn your trust, and they are priceless people to know.

* * *

Neil, who worked tirelessly for me for free, started to get pressure from his company, Thompson Franks, to bring in a return on their time investment. Embarrassed, he confided this to me. In the end he actually said he did not think the investments his company offered would be in David's best interest and that I should leave them. The next time I heard from him he had lost his job; the company cited unprofessionalism as the reason. Having dealt with him, I know that he was among the most professional people I have ever had the pleasure of working with.

Soon after he was replaced, I had a phone call from the company, asking if I would like to come in for a meeting. I let the replacement list all his magnificent achievements before turning down his offer and asking that they never get in touch with me again. I then hired Neil as my personal advisor, although he charges me only for the tax returns and annual accounts, just part of the work involved, and he still performs that role today.

Even now it is a constant struggle to ensure David's money will be there for him for the rest of his life. The money left with the court now pays only 0.5 per cent interest, compared with a few years ago when it paid 6 per cent, making a huge difference to David's quality of life. I feel this is a brutal assault on a member of one of the most vulnerable groups in our society.

12

Shifting sands

Eventually my dealings with the medical and legal professions started to fade into memories as painfully slowly the loose ends became tied up. We managed to find David a flat and I started to pay off my debts. I was mentally, physically and emotionally drained, but remained optimistic. I had developed a toughness of spirit that would protect me and occasionally allow me to retaliate when people tried to pull a fast one.

Finding care for David, however, continued to be quite a task. Care was hired and fired, usually because people took advantage of David and his money or simply failed to understand his condition or to provide the perfect balance of care and companionship that he required. The biggest problem I generally found with people was that they would associate brain damage with learning difficulties although they are not one and the same.

David's intelligence is not diminished – he still has the ability to hold a normal conversation and discuss day-to -day issues – but he has lost the faculties of logic, reasoning and perception. He feels frustrated when others fail to recognise this and this causes much of the problem. People have a habit of referring to David in the third person and not talking to him directly; they spell out what is best for him instead of helping him to work this out for himself, or even trying to become a friend and companion, and gain his trust.

I encountered the same problem when I was working for the nursing agency. Having asked for work in any area that dealt with brain injury and cognitive behavioural rehabilitation, I was left alone in a care-in-the-community home setting with three learning difficulty patients each with hugely varying issues. I was completely out of my depth due to the lack of understanding of the admin staff who had confused brain damage with learning difficulties. Even when I remonstrated with them they still did not understand the difference.

With no training whatsoever, I arrived at the property to find that the previous carer had left without leaving me a key and that three people were disembarking from a minibus and setting off in different directions. A neighbour shouted across to me that these were my patients who were not to be left on their own till eight the next morning and that the key was hidden under a stone. It took me the best part of an hour to round them all up and get them safely inside, and then, as none of them got on, I spent all night keeping the peace. My experience of brain injury had not prepared me enough for work with patients with learning difficulties.

Going back to David's care, much of it fell to John and me. I desperately wanted John to study for his career but it was impossible in our situation then, and he would never have done anything that he felt was letting his brother down. With hindsight, I wish John and I had undergone some sort of counselling, as we were probably in denial about the stress we had been under.

A woman called Diana approached us looking for a role as live-in carer companion for David and, after getting to know her a little, we agreed to give her a trial run. Although she had another job, we struck a deal whereby she would live with David without having to pay any rent or bills, as long as she spent time with him in the evenings and at weekends. Surprisingly, this arrangement has become a success with the continuing support of family and friends.

They got along famously, playing golf and going travelling together. When Diana was made redundant from her job, we decided to make it a permanent arrangement for her to carry on with us. She was overjoyed as she had become a close friend of David's and attuned to his unique needs. At the time of writing, the arrangement is still in place, and she is as one of the family, much better than the various professionals who had at best looked after David half-heartedly.

John has secured a good job in a bank, joining the world of professionals! And as for me, well, despite all the improvements, I still had demons, grudges and regrets. I often thought about trying to sue people, to right wrongs and to try and do my little bit to alter the landscape. But did I need any more stress? And would it be wise to go to the expense and hard work of suing a large legal firm when it could turn out that although it had seemed to act grossly unethically, it had acted just within the boundaries of the law? I sought counsel on this and came to no conclusion.

But then the idea started forming about writing this book. I could get everything off my chest and more importantly I could offer words of warning, and maybe hope, to anyone going through what we have been through.

Not being a writer, I started looking around for someone to pen my story for me. I found an author called Norma who advised me that although it would be very expensive for her to write a book, that if I could write it in a draft form she would be able to re-write it in readable English for a more reasonable sum. With my family settling down, it was the right time to sell up and move David into his own flat, which I did while John and I moved into a small semi nearby. This also freed up some cash for the ghost writer.

Writing those first drafts was more painful than I could ever imagine. I had collected copious notes over the years, but now I tried to work through the story methodically and chronologically so as not to miss out details. This process was like reliving the whole eleven years, recalling feelings as though I was having them at that moment. I could remember with clarity and precision the words people said to me, from throwaway comments to life-shattering declarations. Eventually I managed to write a few chapters and sent them off to Norma to get started.

Within a few days she called asking if I had seen *The Times* that day. She read out an article about a neurosurgeon called Mr Winner who was speaking about the lack of rehabilitative care after brain injury. It was the very person who had told me that David needed no rehabilitation, when everyone else knew he did. I felt relieved that in Norma I had found someone who was interested enough to understand and who would help me tell my story.

***

The years of looking after my sons, especially looking after David, meant that I did not have as much time as I would have liked to spend with my parents as they reached retirement age. Sadly I had been somewhat unaware of their ageing and deterioration, and my father was also to suffer at the hands of incompetent healthcare and social services staff.

For months I tried to help him when he was at home, even though I was also caring for David. Cost-cutting and misdiagnosis led to him being taken to various inappropriate residential homes. The experiences of his last six weeks of life were shocking even by the standards of what David had been through. He had developed a problem with his throat which prevented him from swallowing, which had been diagnosed by his GP but never entered into his records. His carers believed he was just being difficult when he told them he could not eat, because there was nothing on his records.

The hospital X-rayed his chest instead of his throat, and then the radiographers went on strike, which meant a backlog and two-week delay in getting the results, by which time it was too late for my father who was now in a terminal condition with fluid on the lungs. This would ultimately lead to his death, essentially dying of thirst after a nil by mouth sign was put over his bed.

Although I had never been close to my father, I regretted not being there for him at the end, or for my mother either, who was too weak to look after him. Our requests for him to be given a side room where he could die with dignity were rejected, and he finally died of thirst and starvation after days of listening to other patients getting meals and drinks brought to their bedsides. It was traumatic and I wished I could have done more. My experience of the NHS and the social services as a patient, a mother, a carer and a member of staff, gives me little hope that they will improve any time soon.

***

Now my life is brighter. The great positive forces for me are my partner George and my two sons. I owe special thanks to George without whose support and help this book might never have been written. David, whose story has led me from the deepest lows to the dizziest

Shifting sands **195**

highs, continues to progress, steadily, surely and encouragingly, and I am confident that he lives a fulfilling life. Things could have worked out so differently, from moments following that first incident in the shower to the final signature on the settlement. There were many, many missed opportunities, where a wise and considered decision could have changed the course of his life, but it does no good to dwell on this. I would like to think that lessons have been learnt; although deep down I remain pessimistic.

How different David's life would be now is impossible to know, but he has what you would call a normal life: a season ticket for Whitely Athletic, the club he once had a trial for, and a golf handicap of twenty. He travels widely, too, not put off by his fateful trip abroad. He still gets headaches and needs medication for epilepsy, but things are manageable. Most importantly, he is happy, and he tells me so. With his wonderful sense of humour he is a joy to be with.

John did not have the adolescence anyone would have planned but it has made him a strong, mature, caring young man, settled in his own flat and committed to a job he loves. In his work he helps people to the best of his ability to plan for their futures. Feeling that he is at last doing something worthwhile and able to plan his own future gives him a sense of satisfaction and peace of mind he once could only dream of.

He was a victim of the accident too, and his recovery has been long and steady, and is still ongoing. He told me recently that if he had to do everything all over again he would not hesitate, such is his devotion towards his brother and me. I am so grateful for his invaluable support to both of us.

With the passing years I lost contact with Norma, but I was lucky enough to find Charlie, a local ghost writer who understood what I wanted to do, and finally helped me to complete my work. Having completed my story some nine years later, thanks to all the invaluable work from Charlie who has worked through some of his own family problems to get this finished I can probably say at last my job is done. Many thanks to Charlie, and also to Rodney, Trish and their team at Fern House Publications who at last enabled this book to become reality. Perhaps while you are reading it I will be swimming with George in the Mediterranean, and going back to his new holiday home. I hope I have earned a rest, and can enjoy my trips away from home.

I would like to say a heartfelt thanks to all the caring people who have helped David come through his ordeal and given him the opportunity to lead a normal life. There are many such people fighting injustice, and we feel incredibly fortunate to have come across a few of them. A special thanks goes to George without whom this book would not have been written. The times I tried and gave up are too numerous to mention, and without his encouragement I would never have got past the first chapter. George made me feel good about myself, gave me the confidence to get this story written and guided me through when the going got tough.

And now, I have renewed optimism for the future, and feel fortunate that together with George, my partner and soulmate, I look forward to retirement. The future is not panning out as I might have envisaged it; but it is so much better than I would ever have dared to expect.